Evangelism
BY FIRE

Evangelism BY FIRE

IGNITING YOUR PASSION FOR THE LOST

REINHARD BONNKE

with George Canty

WORD PUBLISHING
Dallas · London · Vancouver · Melbourne

EVANGELISM BY FIRE

Unless otherwise indicated, all Scripture quotations are from the King James Version of the Bible. Scriptures identified as NIV are from the New International Version, copyright © 1973, 1978, International Bible Society. Those identified as NKJV are from the New King James Version, copyright © 1979, 1980, 1982, Thomas Nelson, Inc., Publishers. Those identified as RSV are from the Revised Standard Version of the Bible, copyright © 1946, 1952, 1971 by the Division of Christian Education of the National Council of Churches of Christ in the U.S.A. Used by Permission.

Library of Congress Cataloging in Publication Data

Bonnke, Reinhard.
    Evangelism by fire : igniting your passion for the lost / Reinhard
Bonnke.
      p.   cm.
    ISBN 0-8499-3254-8 :
    1. Evangelistic work. 2. Witness bearing (Christianity)
3. Bonnke, Reinhard. I. Title.
BV3790.B59 1990
269' .2 – dc20   90=41596
                                                              CIP

Printed in the United States of America

01239 BA 9 8 7 6 5 4 3 2 1

Dedication

To the inspiring memory of
my unforgettable brothers, friends, and CfaN team workers

Horst Kosanke and Milton Kasselman

who laid down their lives
for the Gospel of Jesus Christ
in Africa,
ascending to glory in chariots of fire,
to receive their crowns of life from the Lord.

Acknowledgment

I wish to acknowledge that my friend and colleague the Reverend George Canty was the collaborating writer of this book. He is a distinguished English author, as well as an international evangelist.

I also thank my friend Jamie Buckingham who has kindly agreed to work on this book with the view of publishing it in North America.

Contents

Foreword

I did not have time to do what Reinhard Bonnke was asking me to do—revise this book for a North American audience. Several years ago I stopped working on books written by other people. I was too busy writing my own. I knew Reinhard and believed in his ministry. On my recommendation a number of people in our church, recognizing the anointing of God on his evangelistic outreach, have sent money to his ministry on a regular basis. But I simply did not have time to go through his manuscript.

Then God whispered in my ear: *Rewrite it for Me.*

I know better than to disobey that sort of command.

Actually, the manuscript was in good shape. But the project was terribly time-consuming and I found myself working early in the morning, late at night, and—using my laptop computer—on cross-country flights.

But something happened to me as I worked with this man's words. I began to catch his spirit—a spirit that burns for lost souls to be won to Jesus. Years ago I had that same spirit. But across the years it had been buried in a lot of other things. Working on this manuscript, however, that slumbering spirit began to come to life. I remembered the words from an old hymn, written by the blind poet Fanny Crosby:

> Rescue the perishing, care for the dying,
> Snatch them in pity from sin and the grave;
> Weep o'er the erring one, lift up the fallen,
> Tell them of Jesus the Mighty to save.

That's why God wanted me to work on this book. Not just to make the manuscript presentable, but to present me, once again, with what has always been the first calling of God: the call to win souls to Jesus.

It is impossible to read these pages without wanting to obey Jesus and become a dynamic personal witness. At the same time, this book exposes the soul and spirit of the man who may be history's greatest individual evangelist.

As I worked with Reinhard's words I found myself praying that the same spirit that lives in him would live in me. Sometimes, sitting at my word processor, deleting words here and adding words there—to clarify meaning—my eyes would fill with tears. When I came to his chapter about the evangelists, missionaries, and martyrs who have gone before, who have sown the seeds of the Gospel in tears, I had to take my fingers off the keys and just sit and listen to God.

"We do not have this harvest," Bonnke writes, referring to the hundreds of thousands who attend his meetings, "because we are superior to those precious men and women [who have gone before], but only because the harvest season has arrived."

He's right. This is the season of the harvest. We do not know how long it will last before the winds of winter once again howl across the earth, slamming shut doors now open. But never in all history have there been so many open doors, so many hearts plowed by adversity ready to receive the good seed of the Gospel. The ability to evangelize, to witness, to win the lost, to carry the Gospel message is not limited to Reinhard Bonnke. Each one of us has that ability. If we obey, as this simple German preacher obeyed, God will use each of us.

This is not a book of methods. It is a book of motivation. Do not read any farther than the bottom of this page unless you are prepared for God to convict your heart and thrust you into a much larger ministry than you ever dreamed. But if that is the desire of your heart—to be an instrument in God's hand—read on. Read slowly. Reread. Even if you are a speed-reader, please do not skim these pages. There is gold to be mined in every sentence.

Reinhard Bonnke is writing so the same spirit that rests on him will rest on you. As the "anointing" was passed from Elijah to Elisha, then on to John the Baptist, to Paul, to the saints, and to the confessors, and on to men like Bonnke—so it is now time for you to be anointed by God for evangelism.

Working on this book has changed my life.

Reading it will change yours.

Jamie Buckingham
Melbourne, Florida

Preface

When I was a young missionary in Africa, I used what others had taught me were the proper methods of missions. Like most other missionaries, I was totally dedicated to my job—but saw few results. My heart, however, longed to see vast multitudes of precious African people rejoicing in Christ. At night I would dream of it—seeing fields and valleys full of hundreds of thousands of Christians standing before God—raising their hands in joyful celebration of His mighty power. The "tried-and-proven" methods of traditional missionary endeavor, however, were only touching a tiny percentage of these people. The way I was doing it was simply not working.

Then God began working on me—with hammer and chisel. I resisted Him at first. Germans, you know, are often like that. But He was even more stubborn than I, and graciously taught me His lessons, one by one.

Then new dimensions of the Holy Spirit began to open. Each one flooded me with astonishment. Signs and wonders began to occur. But each new revelation was costly. There was, I began to understand, no instant formula for success.

This book is filled with the things God has taught me—and allowed me to experience—over the years. I'm writing for one reason alone—to inspire others to evangelism. In this book I have laid out the principles necessary for any Holy Spirit ministry. Read it not to discover how I operate in my evangelism crusades; read it to discover how God operates through anyone willing to follow His plan.

During the time I was writing this book I saw as many as 150,000 people come to salvation in a single meeting—more than two million in a single year. Everywhere I go to preach in Africa the crowds grow larger. Multitudes are being healed and filled with the Holy

Spirit. My early dreams — seeing the plains of Africa filled with multitudes praising God for His mighty power—have come to life. Yet I treasure in my heart what I believe is God's assurance that one day we shall gather in a harvest of one million souls in a single service.   We have seen whole countries shaken by the power of the Gospel of Jesus Christ. If this can be the result of things God has shown me, my hope is that God will show others, also. I pray for you, my reader, that you will have a heart revelation of the matchless glory of His power, a power beyond anything I have ever seen (or anyone else has ever seen, for that matter). The potentials of Pentecost have never yet been fully utilized. There is much more to come.

Two thoughts long have thundered in my soul. First, the vision God gave me of a blood-washed Africa. Second, the principle of plundering hell to populate heaven. These are not mere notions of farfetched ideals, but words from God which He will fulfill. God will not give the whole world to any one man or woman. He wants to raise up *an army* of anointed people.

It is God who creates evangelists out of ordinary flesh-and-blood folk. Angels can never do the job God has given to men, for angels have never known the joy of being saved by grace. Angels operate out of perfect obedience to the Lord. Redeemed men and women operate not only out of obedience—but out of gratitude for what Christ has done for us at Calvary.

The angel who appeared to Cornelius in Acts 10 was not allowed to mention the name of Jesus, nor to speak about salvation to the man. That high and holy privilege was (and is) reserved for men and women—people like you and me. All the angel was allowed to say was, "Now send men to Joppa and call for one Simon, whose surname is Peter . . . "(v. 5). This mighty seraph from deep heaven had to bow to Peter's higher privilege. It pleases God to call and to send people like you and me.

It has always been this way. God used four evangelists—Matthew, Mark, Luke, and John—to write down the story of the Gospel of Jesus Christ. Such a pattern is linked, in my mind, to the four men in Old Testament times who carried the Ark of the Covenant. Carriers of the Gospel change from generation to generation, but the Gospel remains the same. Now we are here, and today it is our turn.

God has called you and me. The Gospel needs to be taken to the ends of the earth. This is the Great Commission of the Lord to us— and the King's business requires haste.

These chapters are written because I do not believe that God's plans call for hell to be bigger than heaven. Although Scripture speaks about "many" who are on their way to eternal destruction (Matt. 7:13), these same people must be intercepted by men and women preaching the original Gospel. Provision has been made to bring "many sons unto glory" (Heb. 2:10); and, praise God, Revelation 7:9 speaks of a successful conclusion.

"Go and make disciples of all nations . . . " (Matt. 28:19, NIV), Jesus instructed. There is no alternate plan in case the Gospel fails. It won't! More people are being saved, healed, and baptized into the Holy Spirit today than ever before in man's history. The tempo is increasing, leading to but one conclusion: Jesus is coming soon.

We are not called to go into a battle with the outcome yet to be decided. The battle was won at Calvary. Our task is to share the victory and the spoils. God's invincible secret is the Cross of Christ, which frightens every demon in hell. Heaven will be an eternal and dominating monument to the victory of the Gospel. These pages are a welcome to join a conquering army, not a plea to support a hopeless and desperate resistance against overwhelming odds. Our Captain never lost a battle—and He never will.

Human schemes are not the answer. If we follow them we will see the present generation die in its sins. The mighty commission of Christ to His church is a call to war against unbelief. Our weapon is the sword of the Gospel.

This is not a book of means and methods, but of spiritual principles. God will give you resourcefulness. There are as many methods as He directs.

We need more imaginative approaches, rather than people doing things by "tried-and-proven" methods — even methods I have tried and proven. Methods which have made little impact in the past are not likely to produce an impact now. Plodding along mechanically might be called faithfulness, but our primary concern in evangelism is effectiveness, not this twisted type of faithfulness.

During my years as an evangelist and missionary I have discovered a number of limiting factors hindering the Gospel. Although I do not address these directly in this book, I know from experience that many of these are the traditional, accepted methods of evangelism which have remained unchanged for generations. Others are doctrines and sentiments which tell us to "leave it all to God." Some insist God's way is revival, but they fail to carry out the Great Commission in the meanwhile. Some think that if people are to be saved, they will be saved anyway.

Suppose such theories are wrong! What an awful risk—to rest the eternal destiny of souls upon a controversial interpretation of a Scripture verse or the turn of a Greek verb. One can be dead right, but dead nonetheless! We dare not neglect the task of evangelism. I would rather use a method despised by man but approved by God, than a method approved by man which gets no results.

It is for this reason I make no apology for this book. I am not writing to be approved by man. I am writing to share God's anointing on all those who are ready to step out in faith. The temperature of this book runs hot—very hot. Its flames will scorch. Some who read these pages would do well to take out fire insurance, for I guarantee many old concepts will be set to the torch.

My message is not one-sided, but it does come from a singleness of heart. I hammer away at the Great Commission, for I know it cannot be over-emphasized. I cry to God day and night for greater effectiveness in winning our generation for Him. *Evangelism by Fire* is the only feasible solution.

I constantly scan the horizons for other anointed men and women who may take up this challenge of the Word of God for Holy-Ghost evangelism. I believe the best is yet to be. The time is coming soon when the whole world will resound with the praises of our God and Savior. In all nations and in every tongue, the day is almost here when every tongue will confess that *Jesus Christ is Lord, to the glory of God the Father.*

Reinhard Bonnke
Frankfurt, Germany

Part 1
The Need

1
The Incendiary Gospel

During World War II many bombers carried what were known as incendiary bombs. These were large bundles of small bombs about the size of one of those cardboard cylinders inside a roll of paper towels. Each bomb had a sharp nose with a tiny detonator and small fins to make it fall straight down; and each was packed with highly flammable material. When released from the planes the bundles would come apart. The little bombs would scatter as they fell, dropping indiscriminately all over the targeted city. Instead of exploding when they hit, however, they were designed to break through the shingles on the roofs of houses and set the attics on fire. Some had delayed-action fuses, meaning they would not set the house on fire until the next day—or the next week. Regardless of when they were activated, though, the bombs had but one purpose—to set things on fire.

The Gospel is a fire-lighter. The Holy Spirit is not given just to help preachers with eloquent sermons. He comes to put a flame in human hearts—just as those incendiary bombs put a flame in the attics of hundreds of houses. Unless Christ sets you alight, you can bring no fire to earth. "Without Me, you can do nothing," He told His disciples (John 15:5, NKJV). Jesus gave specific instructions to His followers as He was departing to ascend into heaven. He told them they were to do nothing until the Holy Spirit came upon them. In fact, they were incapable of performing miracles, healing the sick, casting out demons, even living effective lives until they were filled with the Holy Spirit. But when He, the Holy Spirit, would come they would "receive power," Jesus said in Acts 1:8. This power would give them the ability to witness to the uttermost parts of the earth. It would be evidenced by "tongues of fire" on their heads (Acts 2:3, NIV).

Earlier Jesus had sent the disciples out in pairs (Luke 10:1). That incident reminds me of Samson sending foxes out two by two. Remember how Samson caught the foxes, tied their tails together, and let the animals carry torches in an arson raid on the enemy's corn shocks and vineyards (Judges 15).

Just so, Jesus sent out His disciples two by two as carriers of the divine torch. They were walking incendiaries, scorching the devil's territories with the Gospel fire.

Until the fire falls, evangelism and church activities are boring, routine, and unexciting. Pulpit essays, homilies, or preaching about the national economy is glacial work that puts congregations to sleep. Such preaching has no divine spark to bring combustion to cold congregations. No one goes home ignited.

In contrast, the two men who walked with Jesus down the Emmaus road the afternoon of His resurrection later remarked how their "hearts burned within them" as they talked to Him. I am sure He didn't talk politics to them, nor offer suggestions and advice on how to invest their money. That wouldn't make their hearts burn.

Jesus came speaking about the kingdom of God and "scattering fire on earth." He did not come to plan a holiday picnic. He came to warn His followers about a deadly enemy and to empower them to take authority over it. Satan is a destroyer. Knowing this, the Lord sent out His servants with a warning of physical dangers. "Fear not them which kill the body, but are not able to kill the soul: but rather fear him which is able to destroy both soul and body in hell" (Matt. 10:28). What is mere physical hurt, compared with a life ablaze with the joy and zest of Jesus? What is bodily danger compared with the crown of life or the wonderful work He gives us to do? "Heal the sick, cleanse the lepers, raise the dead, cast out devils: freely ye have received, freely give" (Matt. 10:8).

When Arson Is Not a Crime

Somebody once said that God sets driftwood on fire. Now that's good news. Soggy, old sticks can burn for God, just like Moses' bush did!

As a young missionary I used to pray, "Lord, let me burn out for Thee." But I don't pray that way anymore. I don't want to be an ash heap. I want to be like Moses' bush. I want to burn, but not be consumed. Too many of God's servants are experiencing "burnout," something that happens when we catch on fire and are consumed. I don't want that to happen to me, so now I pray instead, "Let me burn *on* for Thee, dear Lord." The altar flame of our lives should never go out.

Without fire, there is no Gospel. The New Testament begins with fire. The first words anyone said about Christ concerned His "fire ministry." John the Baptist, who himself was called a "burning and shining light," introduced Jesus saying: "He shall baptize you with the Holy Ghost, and with fire: Whose fan is in his hand, and he will throughly purge his floor, and gather his wheat into the garner; but he will burn up the chaff with unquenchable fire" (Matt. 3:11–12).

This was how John the Baptizer introduced Jesus the Baptizer. But Jesus was a different kind of baptizer. John used water, a physical element, but Christ baptized people with the Holy Spirit and fire. Water and fire—what a contrast! While John the Baptist stood in the cold waters of the Jordan River, Jesus stood in a river of spiritual fire.

The notable work of John was baptism. When he announced Jesus, however, he pointed out that the Son of God was also a baptizer. Baptism is the Lord's present great work. Jesus came to baptize in the Holy Spirit. If you are a born-again believer, this is Christ's major experience for you.

The Sign of the Son of Man

Fire is the ensign of the Gospel, the sign of the Son of Man. Only Jesus baptizes in fire. When we see such baptisms, that is the evidence that He, and nobody else, is at work. The baptism of fire is the identifying hallmark of His activity. Put your hand on such

5

activities, and you will feel the heat. The prophet Elijah made the same point when he said, "the God that answereth by fire, let him be God" (1 Kings 18:24).

What does your spiritual thermometer read? Does it even register? Are you chilled? Are the altars in the church cold? Do you worship without warmth? Is the only heat in your church generated by the friction of disputes over doctrines?

Most theologies and teachings are as inflammable as asbestos. There are religious books that provide heat only if put on a bonfire. Many sermons are deliberately fireproof. Such faith-chilling items have nothing to do with the Christ of Pentecost. Whatever He touches catches fire. Jesus melts the ice.

Some church efforts to whip up a little enthusiasm do no more good than rubbing two wet sticks together. They may provide a lot of friction and even some sweat—but no fire. God is dropping His incendiary bombs all over the world. Those who are flammable immediately burst into flames. Those who are wet and soggy from years of hearing a dull Gospel simply let the flame burn out.

Satan's Brain Damage

The fire of God is special—unique. Only the fire of God was allowed on the altar of Moses, not the fire produced by any human means. Defying this law, Nadab and Abihu made fire themselves and lit their incense with it. But divine fire gushed from the tabernacle, swallowed up the "strange fire," and brought death to the two rebel priests (Lev. 10:1–2, NIV).

Today strange fire still is being offered. Strange gospels which are not Gospels at all, but theologies of unbelief, are being taught in many sections of the world. The thoughts of men and their philosophies, criticisms, and theories are not the Gospel. They bear no trace of the glory-heat from heaven. Nothing in them produces any combustion except the controversy they bring.

My friend Paul Schoch once showed me something in the Scripture. He reached over, picked up his Bible, and opened it to Matthew 16, where he read the story of Simon Peter's great confession.

Then Paul pointed out how, just a few moments later, Jesus—after having just commended Peter—called him "Satan": "Get behind me, Satan! You are a stumbling block to me; you do not have in mind the things of God, but the things of men" (Matt. 16:23, NKJV).

This passage shows that thoughts exist on two opposing levels, Paul explained. There are the thoughts of God and the thoughts of men. Isaiah quoted God on this when he said,

> For my thoughts are not your thoughts, neither are your ways my ways . . . . For as the heavens are higher than the earth, so are my ways higher than your ways, and my thoughts than your thoughts. (Isa. 55:8–9)

Just that one small thought helped me understand many things about God and man. For instance, Satan thinks as humans think. The fact is, Satan simply cannot understand God's mind. That is strange when you remember that he was originally Lucifer, a throne angel of God. When Jesus bruised the serpent's head, I think He inflicted some kind of brain damage upon the devil! Once Satan was full of wisdom; today he is disoriented. That prince of the power of the air is baffled by what God is doing, especially by what the Lord did at the Cross. This type of confusion is spread by sin into the minds of men and women; it runs through the human race as a horrible infection.

When I say Satan thinks as humans think, I actually mean that humans think as the devil thinks. In short, he plants his confusion about God in their minds so that they, too, find the Cross a relic of foolishness. They cannot grasp the things of God.

The apostle Paul, writing to the Christians in Corinth, confessed that at first he also could not understand the message of the Cross. His reaction to the Gospel message was cold fury against the believers. It ate away his heart, and he became a "dragon man," breathing out threats and slaughter. Full of zeal, his brain was full of clever unbelief. He was thinking the same way Satan thought—thoughts of confusion about the plan of God. Then, three days following his conversion, he was baptized in the Holy Spirit. The moment that happened scales fell from his eyes. Suddenly he could not only see—he could understand. The Holy Spirit gave him the "mind of Christ," and he was able to think as God thinks, no longer as Satan thought.

I wonder if hell would like to send espionage agents into the kingdom of God, just to see what secrets are there. Yet, even if such spies did arrive, they would be like the Satan-thinking spies sent out by Moses on the scouting trip into Canaan. Those spies, you remember, did not have the mind of God. They saw the challenges of the Promised Land as bigger than the promises of God. Only Joshua and Caleb understood God's thoughts, insisting the children of Israel could conquer the giants and the walled cities—not because they were stronger than the giants, but because God had said it would be so.

So, even if hell sent espionage agents into heaven, they still wouldn't understand these secrets, for they are hidden from all except those who have the mind of Christ. Hell remains baffled by Christ's sacrifice at Calvary. It sees salvation as a deep-laid plot devised by God for His own advantage and His own glory. He has deliberately hidden its secrets from the devil for He knows Satan devours others—that is his evil nature.

If we are to fight the devil on the level of human thought, we must remember that he thinks as humans think. Satan invented a human chess game, and has played it for ten thousand years. He has experience from the time of Adam onward. The devil anticipates our every move; he will checkmate us ten miles ahead. He knows every trick of human ingenuity. He knows, for instance, that you cannot produce faith by the wisdom of words. The devil always has a counter statement for whatever you say. Therefore, anything said or done from the perspective of man's wisdom is useless in spiritual warfare.

The Gospel didn't come out of somebody's head. A brilliant university professor didn't dream it up and give it to the world. To understand the Gospel we must move into the divine dimension. Only there are we protected, because the enemy cannot follow us there. The devil is no match for the mind of the Holy Spirit. If we plan, preach, witness, and evangelize as human beings, Satan will foil us. He can handle psychology and propaganda. Instead, the answer to all our dilemmas is this: Move in the Spirit and preach the Gospel as it is.

Then the arch-confuser becomes confused. Then he can't follow the game at all. The devil doesn't even know the Holy Spirit's alphabet.

I see this constantly in our Gospel crusades across Africa. We completely open the meetings to the Holy Spirit. We welcome Him into our meetings even though we never know what He may bring. Where false religion and doctrines of demons previously have prevailed, they are shaken and broken. The results are always thrilling. Entire countries are challenged by the mighty power of Christ. No preacher could do this, no matter how popular or clever. Such success happens only when God does it His way. When He enters the field, there is a mighty victory. He can, will, and *does* succeed. All we have to do is allow Him to take over.

These breakthroughs are part of the end-time blessings the Lord promised. The Day of Pentecost continues. It did not stop at Jerusalem in the first century. Peter, preaching on that marvelous day, said, "The promise is for you and your children and for all who are far off—for all whom the Lord our God will call" (Acts 2:39, NKJV).

I offer this challenge: All who operate on the level of the Spirit will see the powerful results. They will see revival come. That kind of evangelism will break Satan's back worldwide, and he will be routed. This is the holy fire which cannot be imitated.

Live Ammunition and a Full Head of Steam

A gun loaded with blanks bangs exactly the same as a gun loaded with live ammunition. A slight difference can be felt in recoil, but not in the noise. The most noticeable difference is that dummy ammunition makes no mark on the target, while a gun loaded with real bullets can hit its mark. Bang and recoil count for nothing unless the bullet hits the mark.

Those of us in true Gospel ministry are not interested in mere bang and recoil. Excitement and spectacular Gospel displays might draw hundreds of thousands of people, but size and noise don't count. We need to see something alive hit the bull's-eye. The crowds may come, but we must let loose a true broadside of Holy-Spirit fire power in order for something to be accomplished. God measures results, not activity. The only thing that counts is whether multitudes are born again, lives are completely changed, churches are filled, hell is plundered, and heaven is populated. Those are results! Hallelujah!

The fire of God is not sent just for the enjoyment of a few emotional experiences. I praise God that His fire has that glorious side effect. Holy-Ghost power produces lively meetings. But just being "happy and clappy" does not satisfy God's design. The Holy Spirit works for eternal purposes.

I think of this when I travel across Africa and see an old steam engine puffing away on a narrow-gauge railroad. These iron horses are like living creatures, breathing steam, and filled with fire in their bellies. The fireman's job is to stoke the fire and get a full head of steam going. When the steam pressure is up, the engineer can do one of two things. He can either pull the whistle cord, or he can turn the lever that directs power onto the pistons. The whistle will blow off steam until there's none left, making itself heard for miles around. If the steam is directed onto the pistons, however, its power will turn the wheels. Steam to the pistons, unlike steam to the whistle, draws no attention to itself; but it enables the train to roll, easily carrying its heavy load across the land.

Thank God for train whistles. They warn us that a train is approaching. They tell us it is time to get aboard. They signal the trainmen to do certain tasks. Whistles are important. But if blowing a whistle was all the steam could do, making a fire under the boiler and stoking it up wouldn't be worthwhile.

Like a locomotive's full head of steam, the fire of the Holy Spirit brings power. Never mind the noise—let us apply this power to get on the move. Thunder is justified, but remember it happens only *after* the lightning has struck. The proper purpose of Pentecost is to get the wheels rolling for God in every church, thereby transporting the Gospel across the face of the whole earth.

The simple commission of Jesus has not changed: "Go into all the world and preach the good news to all creation" (Mark 16:15, NIV). The church is to be a *going* church, not a *sitting* church. We are called to look *outward* to where our Lord is moving across the continents, not *inward,* forever examining our own souls. Those who look inward are incapacitated by introspection. Jesus says to them: "Don't worry. I have saved you. Now it is time to start helping save others."

The Holy Ghost has come, and it is time to be up and going. He does the work—not you or I. "Woe is me if I preach not the gospel," Paul said in 1 Corinthians 9:16, NKJV. And woe are we if we do not join in that same task!

The Fire Age

Let me ask a question: Why was Jesus exalted to the right hand of God? I have read the greatest of commentaries, and virtually nothing is written on that subject. Christ's ascension is a neglected study. Is it of such little importance? Jesus, talking about His own ascension to heaven, said it was of great importance. "But I tell you the truth: It is for your good that I am going away. Unless I go away, the Counselor will not come to you; but if I go, I will send him to you" (John 16:7, NIV). Jesus said that unless He went to the Father, a most essential experience would never be ours. Without the Lord's ascension, we could never be baptized into the Spirit.

Look back upon all that Jesus did. John writes that His works were so many that, if they were all written, the whole world could not contain the books. So what could there be that He could not do while He was on earth? There was one thing. It was the very thing which John the Baptist said He would do—baptize in fire and in the Holy Spirit. That's what he couldn't do when He was on earth. Jesus came from heaven and had to return there via the Cross and the empty tomb before the final part of His mission could begin. Nothing Jesus did on earth could be described as baptizing with the Holy Spirit and with fire. In none of His mighty works—His preaching, His teaching, His healing, or in His death and resurrection—did He say He was baptizing with the Holy Spirit. Jesus did much for His disciples; He gave them authority to carry out healing missions. But He went away without baptizing them into the Holy Ghost.

Yet John the Baptist promised that Jesus *would* baptize all His followers in the Holy Spirit. It was that promise Jesus referred to just moments before He ascended into heaven, when He commanded His followers, "Do not leave Jerusalem, but wait for the gift my Father promised, which you have heard me speak about. For John baptized with water, but in a few days you will be baptized with the Holy Spirit" (Acts 1:4–5, NIV).

Such a baptism could not have happened until He went to the Father. Indeed, the Lord not only said it, He emphasized it. *He entered glory to take up this brand new office,* the office of the Baptizer in the Holy Spirit. This is the reason He ascended to the Father. The writers of the Old Testament knew nothing of such a baptism. It was God's "new thing." Jesus brings us many other blessings now, of course. He is our High Priest, our Advocate, our Intercessor, our Representative. But He Himself did not name these works. Other biblical writers pointed these things out in describing Him. The only continuing task that Jesus described for Himself was the task of baptizing His followers in the Holy Spirit.

When He did ascend, and not before, the Spirit came to the apostles as "tongues of fire . . . came to rest on each of them" (Acts 2:3, NIV). This was not a new experience in history—but it was extremely rare. The altar in the tabernacle of Moses and in the temple of Solomon had been set ablaze by the pure fire from heaven. Elijah had prayed on Mt. Carmel and fire had come from heaven and consumed his sacrifice. The flames in the upper room of Pentecost came from the same heavenly source. Jesus has all power at His command. He is in the control room.

Tongues of Fire

What does it mean that the present work of Jesus is to baptize into the Holy Spirit? It means that everything that has to do with the Gospel message, with the ministry of the church, with the ministry of evangelism is to be characterized by fire. Everything that God touches should burn—without being consumed. There should be fire in those who witness and work. Fire in those who preach. Fire in the truth we preach.

"Is not my word like fire . . . ?" God asks in Jeremiah 23:29 (NIV). Earlier Jeremiah had declared, after trying to resign from the ministry, that he could not because "his word is in my heart like a fire" (Jer. 20:9, NIV).

In another example, the writer of Hebrews, after warning the Jewish Christians in the first century that everything on earth was going to be shaken, reminded them that "Our God is a consuming fire" (Heb. 12:29, NIV). And remember that it was the anointing of the Holy Spirit in "tongues of fire" which enabled Peter to preach at Pentecost, resulting in three thousand being saved (Acts 2:3).

Consider these things:

1. All Sacrifice Must Be Consumed by Fire. Two sacrifices were offered on Mount Carmel. One was offered by the priests of Baal, the other by Elijah. It amounted to a contest since Elijah had challenged the priests of Baal as to which God—Baal or Jehovah—would send fire to consume the sacrifices. The sacrifice to Baal never burned; it was fireless. The sacrifice meat was there on the altar. The sacrificers were intensely earnest. They prayed to Baal all day. They cut themselves with knives to show how desperate their sincerity was. They put everything they had into it, yet their sacrifice brought no fire. If the devil could have brought up a spark from hell to make a blaze, Satan would have; but the altar stayed cold.

Fire did not fall simply because Elijah set up a sacrifice, however. It came when Elijah prayed and believed. True, Elijah had to put things in order. He had to prepare the altar and provide the sacrifice. Actually, in doing this he followed to the letter the instructions Moses gave on how to prepare an altar. But obedience to the law was not enough to bring the fire. It was his faith which kindled the blaze.

Sometimes people pray for fire but get no answer, because they are not yielded to God. They aren't willing to provide the necessary sacrifice. They are not willing to sacrifice time or money. They want answers, but they render no effort. They want God's fire so they can sit around and warm themselves beside it. But armchair Christians receive no fire. God does not send His fire to make us comfortable. Nor does His fire come to save us from trouble in our ministry. Quite the opposite: The fire often brings additional trouble with it. Sometimes, as ungodly preachers have learned, the fire burns those who call it down. Children should not play with fire.

It is the fire that matters, however. Setting up a sacrifice is not enough. True, God won't save souls and heal the sick until we lay our all on the altar for Him. But God does not send His fire because we sacrifice. He performs His wonders of salvation and healing because of His mercy and grace. Elijah's godliness did not generate the awesome lightning that burned up everything on the altar. The fire did not come because of his holiness. Tithes and offerings cannot buy even a tiny candle flame of the celestial fire. The fire of God comes, not because of *our* sacrifice, but because of *Christ's* sacrifice. That means, however, the fire is for all. Thank God!

Revival fire is not a reward for good people. It is God's gift to any who believe in it. Why struggle for it? People talk about "paying the price." But there is no need to pay a great deal for what is given freely. Fire comes by faith—alone.

2. Truth Needs to Be Fire-baptized. We can be dead right, but dead nonetheless. We can insist on the "body of truth," but that body may be a cold corpse. Jesus did not merely say, "I am the way and the truth." He said, "I am the way and the truth and the *life*" (John 14:6, NIV, emphasis added).

God also said He would "create over all of Mount Zion and over those who assemble there . . . a glow of flaming fire . . . " (Isa. 4:5, NIV). And Jesus testified that John the Baptist was a "lamp that burned and gave light" (John 5:35, NIV).

All these are images of light and heat. Even though the silly world may smile and snicker at our preaching, the Gospel we preach is a hot Gospel. It burns away chaff and all falsehood.

People sometimes accuse me of being loud and lively when I preach. But I do not know how to preach the "lively oracles" of God (Acts 7:38) without being lively. The Gospel is about fire. To preach the Gospel coolly and casually would be ridiculous.

One day a lady told me there was a "demon" sitting on her, although she was a born-again Christian. I said to her, "Flies can only sit on a cold stove, and on a cold stove they can sit very long! Get the fire of the Holy Spirit into your life, and that dirty demon will not dare to touch you, lest he burn his filthy fingers."

The Gospel provides its own fiery power—its own power of deliverance. It is like some of the new kitchen ovens—it is self-cleaning. There can be no demonic crust, or even residue, when the fire of the Holy Spirit burns in your oven. And that's the reason I'm excited all the time. It is natural for a preacher to be fired up.

In human experience, God's fire translates into passion, the type of passion we saw in Jesus. When Jesus was going to Jerusalem for the last time, He walked ahead of His disciples—urging Himself on. Mark describes the situation: "They were on their way up to Jerusalem, with Jesus leading the way, and the disciples were astonished, while those who followed were afraid" (Mark 10:32, NIV). The fire in His soul was evident even in the way He walked.

When they arrived in Jerusalem and Jesus saw the desecration of the temple, His reaction turned Him into an awesome figure. Seeing Him as He cleansed the temple with a whip made of ropes, overturning the tables of the moneychangers with fire flashing from His eyes, the disciples were reminded of the words of Psalm 69:9, (NIV): "for zeal for your house consumes me." Yet His anger was fueled by His love, not some kind of cold fury. Jesus wasn't a frenzied fanatic. He loved His Father's house, that's all. It was His desire to see people in the temple, worshiping with freedom and happiness. Instead He saw the cheap commercialism—and His heart overflowed like a volcano. When the fire in His soul made Him cleanse the temple, His actions were frightening. Yet as we read the story it was only the moneychangers who fled. The children, the blind, and the lame stayed behind, and He healed them.

A Museum of Marble Figures

God has but one message, and it is a burning message. He doesn't need fireworks. Firebrands don't need to be hotheads. Everything about the church, however, should reflect the warm light of God. This is true from the highest steeple ("In His temple all cry, 'Glory!'"

Ps. 29:9, NIV) to the leaders of the flock (God makes "His ministers a flame of fire," Heb. 1:7, NKJV). His people should be torches. Not only evangelists, but all believers should glow with the Holy Ghost, like torches in a dark street.

A fish has the same temperature as the water in which it swims. Too many Christians are like that—they have no more warmth of spirit than the cold, unbelieving world around them. Human beings, however, are warm-blooded creatures. That is the way the Lord made us. We are designed and chosen to change the temperature around us because of the fire that burns within us. That means the church business meeting should be just as fired by the Holy Spirit as the revival meeting—perhaps even more so.

The Lord does not send us out because we have cool heads and dignity. Nor does He choose us because of our self-composure. He sends us out as live coals from the altar, as witnesses to the Resurrection, to testify that we have met the God of Pentecost. I've heard sermons that were like lectures on embalming the dead. Such talk reminds no one of the living Jesus. Neither Jesus, Peter, nor Paul left congregations sitting like marble statues in a museum. Their messages brought life to dead bodies, fire to cold embers.

Logic can be set alight and still be logic, like the logic of Isaiah or Paul, for example. "Come now, let us reason together," God said to His people. Reason is pure logic. But what are we to be logical about? The rest of that verse sets the logic on fire: "Though your sins are like scarlet, they shall be as white as snow; though they are red as crimson, they shall be like wool" (Isa. 1:18, NIV). Logic need not belong to the glacial period. *Fire implies fervor, not ignorance.* God wants us to learn, to be educated and logical, but our logic should give additional fuel to the fire, not put it out. Remember—radiance before cleverness. Jesus told the rich young ruler he should love God not only with his heart and soul, but with his *mind* also. The Lord wants us to have a warm heart—filled with joy, gusto, and love.

Human dignity takes on a new meaning when people are rapt in praise to God. I wish everyone of you reading this book could have the privilege that is so often mine, to stand on a platform before a huge sea of humanity in Africa and see 150,000 people weeping, waving, jumping, and shouting in gladness to God. What else would you expect to happen when a mother stands on our platform, testifying that her child has just been healed of congenital blindness or deafness, or of twisted limbs? Over and over I have seen these miracle testimonies. It is a glorious scene, the height of human experience. It is no wonder I am excited. How can I keep silent when I see the power of God fall in such force and frequency?

Would you expect me to keep perfectly cool as the lame walk and the blind see? Such reserve isn't clever—it is stupid. I dance, and so does everyone else who witnesses these miracles. That's more in keeping with such moments. In the presence of the Lord there is joy. Jesus said that if we didn't rejoice at such times, even the stones would cry out.

So many times I look at the precious men and women, black or white, many who were so sad earlier, standing in one of our meetings, hands pressed together in emotion or lifted high in worship, eyes glistening with glad tears, faces turned up to God, lips moving in wonder and thankfulness. I say to myself, *how beautiful they are!* and I weep with them as I join their dance of joy. When dignity comes before our delight in God, that is a catastrophe!

If God does not touch our feelings, the devil will. How can God convict sinners and help them come to repentance unless they feel moved? How can He grant them the joy of sins forgiven, without giving them any sensation in their souls? The job of the evangelist is to light a fire in the human spirit—a fire fueled by the Holy Spirit. I am but a match-striker. The rest is up to God.

The results of salvation are even more exciting than the events leading up to it. It caused a lame man to go dancing and leaping into the temple. It caused a street woman to wash the feet of Jesus with her tears. It caused a stingy tax collector to throw an extravagant party. It caused Mary Magdalene to break open a box of spikenard worth a small fortune and anoint the feet of Jesus. It caused Zaccheus to give away lots of money.

Rejoice in undertones? Worship in whispers? Participate in silent celebrations? That is not what the word "rejoice" means. It means "to exult, shout, be rapturous." That's what fire does to us.

The fire of the Holy Spirit is real. It must flow through the church of Jesus Christ like blood through the veins. There is but one call— to be on fire for God. When that happens among Christians, we will win our lost generation for Him.

2

The Last Hour

Suppose you had one hour left to live. How would you spend it? What a flurry of anxious preparations there would be! But let me tell you, it *is* the last hour. It's just that God's method of measuring hours is different—and unknown to us.

"Dear children," the apostle John wrote, "this is the last hour"(1 John 2:18, NIV). When we look at our calendars it seems this "last hour" has lasted a long time—almost two thousand years, in fact. But don't let that confuse you. One thing is certain: If it was the last hour *then*, it most certainly is the last hour *now!* If John were writing today he most certainly would write: "Dear children, it is the last second of the last hour."

When John wrote those words he was watching God's clock, not ours. The hands on God's clock have not stood still. The question we all must face, then, is how long will God's hour last, as measured by earthly timekeeping methods? The one thing we *do* know is that we *don't* know how near we are to the end.

Jesus often spoke of the last hour. Once He said, "No one knows about that day or hour, not even the angels in heaven, nor the Son, but only the Father" (Matt. 24:36, NIV). It is obvious, however, that we are much closer to the end every day. Paul saw it that way, too:

> And do this, understanding the present time. The hour has come for you to wake up from your slumber, because our salvation is nearer now than when we first believed. The night is nearly over; the day is almost here. (Rom. 13:11–12, NIV)

If you knew you had only sixty minutes left, you certainly would not spend the time on trivialities. With the sands running out, things would come into clear focus and you would see what was really important to you. You would not go shopping for the latest fashionable clothes, or run an eye down the financial columns to see how your stocks were doing. Focusing on the end would radically change your outlook and put all of life into its proper perspective.

Somebody once said that most people live as if this life were a permanent arrangement. The Bible's message is that our days are numbered—not numberless. There is time left only for the important things.

I often consider this concept when I think about the church of Jesus Christ. People often tell me I am too simplistic—that life consists of a thousand details. But minor details must never outweigh major concerns. And there is but one major concern as far as the church is concerned. The church's task is simple: *To wage war against Satan in the campaign for souls.*

The great quality of Jesus is that He came when the Father sent Him. And the great quality about us should be that we go when Jesus sends us. "As the Father has sent me, I am sending you" (John 20:21, NIV). The church should never let anything interfere with Jesus' command to go.

Last-Hour Logic

The Bible's insistence that this is the last hour is a unique and special doctrine of Scripture called "imminence." Many ease back into thinking *there are still four months to harvest.* Yet when we look at the apostle Paul and see how much he accomplished in such a short time, we realize he literally lived out what he wrote to the church at Corinth:

> The time is short. From now on those who have wives should live as if they had none; those who mourn, as if they did not; those who are happy, as if they were not; those who buy something, as if it were not theirs to keep; those who use the things of the world, as if not engrossed in them. For this world in its present form is passing away. (1 Cor. 7:29–31, NIV)

Paul lived as if the end of all things was at hand, as if the dropping of the final curtain was always imminent.

The Gospel is eternal, but we don't have eternity to preach it. Yet when we view the often leisurely operations of the church it's as if Christians think there is no hurry, no crisis about to happen, no sense of desperation. We have only as long as we live to reach those who live while we are alive. At present, over five billion souls are living. They are living in our present world, not in an indefinite future age which needs to be evangelized. *It is the last hour!*

Run!

To make sure the Prodigal Son was welcomed home properly, the father *ran!* In his zeal, he ran! I have wanted to run, too, since the Holy Spirit charged my soul with this realization: It is the last hour. The world's airlines have found me a good customer. Why? Because I take seriously Jesus' command to "Go into all the world and preach the Gospel."

One of Paul's favorite Greek words was *spoude*, meaning "to stretch out your neck as a man running to reach the finish line." It is translated "be diligent, study, be earnest, hasten, be zealous, be forward."

I take that literally. I believe God wants me to be all those things in my quest for lost souls. It is sad, tragic, that the church does not seem to feel this sense of zealousness. Instead of stretching out its neck to break the wire at the finish line, it is sitting on the sidelines strumming on its harp and watching the parade go by.

Many churches are very active—but active doing what? To fiddle about with secular issues is one way to look impressively busy and "relevant." But the only true relevance is to bring the Gospel to a dying world.

Giving all our thoughts to our personal spirituality when the fires of hell have broken out, is like members of the fire brigade having a shave before answering a fire call. We can spend years "standing for our principles" when we are only justifying our church quarrels and prejudices. The command to evangelize is all that matters—snatching men from the flames.

That divine command was not given by the Lord in a passing mood. God Himself is driven by the peril in which human beings stand without Christ. Calvary was His imperative! "I have other sheep that are not of this sheep pen. I must bring them also" (John 10:16, NIV).

Walking with His disciples on the Emmaus Road Jesus told them that it "behoved Christ to suffer" (Luke 24:46). The same Greek word, *dei*, is used in both these sayings of Christ. The word does not mean that it was fitting or proper for Him to suffer, but that He *had* to do so—that it was in Him to do it.

The God who went to the Cross did not do so to give us a hobby or an interest for our leisure time. Our Lord did not die to provide a minor occupation for a few church folk. He commands us to preach the Gospel to every creature. This task *needs* us all. As Jesus was *compelled* to go to the cross to save mankind, so we should be *compelled* to witness to others of His great love. We deceive ourselves and lose the inner meaning of the Word of God if we think that this "last hour" is not upon us. It is! It is no use saying, "God's last hour is a pretty long one, so why hurry?" We have only today. In the most intense meaning of the word, it *is* the last hour.

John may have written it long centuries ago, but he was right. There was no hiccup in his inspiration. All mankind stands with toenails hanging over the abyss of eternity.

- It is the last hour of opportunity in many a place.

- It is the last hour of possibility to obey the command of the Lord when He said, "Go ye into all the world . . . ."

- It is the last hour before Jesus returns.

Paid by the Hour

Years ago in northern Germany, I had the privilege of leading an elderly lady to the Lord. For most of her life she had been a church organist, yet she had never known Jesus as her own Savior. When she heard the Gospel and opened her heart to the Lord, she was overwhelmed with the joy of the Holy Spirit. Three days later I met her again, but this time she was completely broken. Puzzled, I asked her why she was that way when I expected her to be filled with joy.

With tears in her eyes, she told me. "I am already seventy years of age and have only just received Jesus as my Savior. I may live perhaps another five or ten years, but I have totally wasted seventy."

I was deeply touched. "Yes," I agreed, "but I know what is going to happen. One day you shall stand before the judgment seat of Christ. And He will not be as concerned about how *long* you cut the furrow of your life for Him, as *how deep*. Ten years out of eighty, on fire for Jesus, is better than living all your life as a lukewarm Christian."

Jesus once told a parable about laborers in a vineyard. By the clock, some had worked only a single hour, but the farmer generously rewarded them, paying them the same as those who had labored all day long. Why? Because they had worked as long as they had the chance to work. This is the principle of God.

If you are worried about not having been at Jesus' side in the harvest when you could have been, the answer is to leave that with the Lord of the harvest. Don't waste time on tears for a past life wasted. *From this moment on, give God wholeheartedly what is His due!* The apostle Paul's advice is this: "Forgetting those things which are behind. . . . Press toward the mark for the prize of the high calling of God in Christ Jesus" (Phil. 3:13–14). As long as you have breath within you, you are in time for the last hour. You are not too late for that.

Young people have a slightly different status in the same last hour, however. When an old person is saved, a soul gets saved. When a young person is saved, both a soul *and* a lifetime are saved. The young person has an hour which could be a lifetime, and what a glorious hour that can be! An hour full of love, joy, peace, purpose, and security, even if that last hour lasts an entire lifetime. The only way to *live tomorrow is to live in faith and activity for Jesus today.*

I once prayed for an old and dying man. As I was praying a strange thought raced through my mind: *What would you pray if you were in his place?* I was reminded of a famous politician who, when asked about his last wish as he lay dying, called for "one of Bellamy's pork pies!" *Is that what I would pray for,* I wondered, *something good to eat?*

It didn't take long before I knew the answer for myself. I would ask the Lord to give me the strength and help to conduct *one more Gospel crusade!* I would like to hit the bull's-eye once more, to once more lead 100,000 souls to the foot of the Cross. There is nothing grander than that, nor is there a more glorious way to die—than fighting on that victorious battleground.

Glorious Crescendo!

The thought of the year 2000 was much in the minds of nineteenth-century believers. For them, the coming of the twentieth century strongly suggested Christ's soon return. Those Christians prayed for new power to evangelize the whole world within one hundred years. The goal of world evangelization was often on their minds, and the thought filled them with much longing.

Now that same thought is filling the minds and hearts of Christians all over the world as we approach the year 2000. Millions of Christians are beginning to pray, asking God for power to see the world evangelized by the end of this decade.

Is it possible? Of course—but only if enough people catch the same vision.

Marine scientists tell us that ocean waves travel thousands of miles, even under the surface and across apparently calm stretches. Approaching land, they develop a majestic crescendo, hunch their mighty shoulders, and build up in rapid momentum and volume to burst finally and magnificently upon the shore. Likewise, a glorious swell of Holy-Ghost power is gathering to a spontaneous crescendo today. It is worldwide, as if hurrying to the shore. The lifting of the waves proves that the shore cannot be far. Jesus is coming soon! *It is the last hour!*

The latter-day Pentecostal outpouring of the Spirit began in 1901 when the truth of the baptism in the Holy Spirit was recovered with signs following. Since then the mightiest revival of all time has swept onward, like a wave from heaven.

That same tidal wave started in Jerusalem nineteen hundred years ago as a divine deluge of power, sending "floods upon the dry ground." It blessed the world for almost three hundred years with continuous revival. Then, because of unbelief and worldliness the wave diminished. The church grew powerless and began teaching that Holy-Ghost power was only for the apostles and the early disciples—as if only they needed it! The Holy Ghost became a mere third article of the creed, locked up and relegated to the past.

Now, however, the wave is back again—roaring toward shore as we approach the end of the century. Once more God's people are on fire all over the world, and once more miracles are taking place, this time with even greater quantity and quality than in the last century.

Anointed for the Last Hour

With this wonderful outpouring of His Spirit, the Lord has given believers the power to do the job. As in the early church, we are once again evangelizing and sending out missionaries. This fulfills John's statement:

> Dear children, this is the last hour; and as you have heard that the antichrist is coming, even now many antichrists have come. This is how we know it is the last hour.
>
> But you have an anointing from the Holy One, and all of you know the truth. . . . Who is the liar? It is the man who denies that Jesus is the Christ. Such a man is the antichrist.
>
> As for you, the anointing you received from him remains in you. . . .
> (1 John 2:18, 20, 22, 27, NIV)

The church is being anointed for the last hour. The spirit of this age, however, is the spirit of *antichrist* or *anti-anointed.* The anointing of the Holy Spirit is a theme which threads its way through the entire book of First John. The apostle's warnings concerning the last times have come home to us today. They strike us with an almost frightening truth about our times. The spirit of antichrist permeates human thinking and society, causing moral collapse. Hostile elements are raging worse and worse, like the early moments of a gathering storm. It is indeed the last hour.

God has His answer, however—the anointing for an anti-anointed latter day. He will never allow the devil to get the upper hand. The outpouring of the Spirit is His special provision for the last hour, described in Joel 2:28–31. "It shall come to pass afterward that I will pour out my spirit upon all flesh. . . . before the great and terrible day of the Lord come." Christ's whole body on earth will be mobilized and armed for the last onslaught of the enemy. The devil will lose again, for Satan is the eternal loser.

Bible Prophecies Are History in Advance

This is the time of ripening for the final harvest. Both wheat and tares fill the field. Satan can see his opportunities are slipping away—it is now or never for him. So the greatest display of wickedness, lawlessness, and degradation is just ahead. But believers have more to think about than mere survival. There are likely to be persecutions, and no doubt blood will flow. Our thoughts, however, are on triumph and conquest for Jesus. The buildup of enemy forces is being more than matched by an ever-increasing measure of the Holy Spirit. "When the enemy shall come in like a flood," Isaiah wrote, "the Spirit of the Lord shall lift up a standard against him" (Isa. 59:19).

The greatest outpouring, the greatest anointing of God's power ever known in history, is coming upon us. Past revivals will seem as nothing when Pentecost breaks upon the entire church. We get glimpses of it already—the battle of the anointed against the anti-anointed. We now know what it means in Revelation 12:11: "And they overcame him by the blood of the Lamb, and by the word of their testimony: and they loved not their lives unto the death." The showdown leading up to that victory is fully described in Revelation 12:9–10, (NIV):

> The great dragon was hurled down—that ancient serpent called the devil or Satan, who leads the whole world astray. He was hurled to the earth, and his angels with him.
> Then I heard a loud voice in heaven say:
> "Now have come the salvation and the power and
> the kingdom of our God,
> and the authority of his Christ.

> For the accuser of our brothers,
>> who accuses them before our God day and night,
>> has been hurled down."

Bible prophecies like these are not alterable. *They are history written in advance!* While the devil is out to trouble the world, God will trouble the devil. God will do what He said He would, even to the dot on the last "i." Hallelujah! We rejoice! We know! The future is settled beforehand, and the last hour is determined, with its own glorious conclusion. *And this is the period we are now entering!*

In our great African Gospel crusades, there are victories over satanic powers and over sorcery. I have seen gigantic piles of witchcraft materials brought together and burned when the owners of these demonic items have been delivered from satanic fears and oppressions by receiving Jesus as their Lord and Savior. I often have pointed to the flames, saying to the crowds, "That is like the final home of the devil—a lake of fire!"

Despite the silly drawings of worldly artists, Satan is not in control of hell's fire. Those flames are his judgment. When those "works of the devil" are reduced to ashes, we then see the true fire of the Lord fall on crowds "en masse." Nothing of the old serpent is left.

The anti-anointing is a strange fire of destruction and of death. But the flame from the presence of the Lord will devour it, just as it devoured the strange fire of Nadab and Abihu. After that, a sweet anointing of peace shall flow over the church, all the way down to its feet.

Let us forget the old fights among God's people over issues which do not lead to the salvation of men and women. Our enemy is not another denomination. Our enemy is not even denominationalism. Our enemy is the devil, and the lies by which he deceives the world.

- The lie that God is dead.

- The lie that God is indifferent.

- The lie that God is powerless.

- The lie that He no longer pours out His Spirit with signs and wonders following.

- The lie that we can do without God.

"They overcame him by the blood of the Lamb" (Rev. 12:11). Note that "him" is singular! We have one enemy—the devil. There is one power to oppose him—the anointing of the Holy Spirit. The anointing breaks the yoke (Isa. 10:27).

3
Mortal Men Can Do Immortal Work

A man with a mission needs vision. Isaiah and Jeremiah had a vision. Without it they would have quit soon after they started. A call from God costs us nothing. To respond to that call, however, is another matter. And to continue in the call could cost us everything. A natural man will soon give up his call unless he is empowered supernaturally. But once that happens, then even a natural man can do the supernatural work of God.

I was a hard-working missionary in Lesotho in Africa, doing the work of God the way missionaries had done it for a hundred years. But I could not shake the dream of a blood-washed Africa. Despite how hard I tried to put it aside, the vision grew more persistent and vivid. It was an all-consuming desire for mass evangelism. I dreamed, time and time again, of hundreds of thousands of Africans in stadiums and open fields, giving their hearts to Jesus Christ. It finally drove me to make my first ventures toward accomplishing my goal. But the members of the German mission board under which I worked disapproved. They were good, spiritual men who meant well; but they were also men without this vision.

Karl Barth once wrote, "Faith is never identical with piety." These men were pious, but they lacked faith. They believed the only acceptable approach to the salvation of Africa was through traditional means—not mass evangelism. Why, they asked, did I think I could do it differently? If mass evangelism was God's way, why were other men not doing it? Who was I, a young German missionary, to believe God had spoken to me and given me a method different from theirs?

I felt isolated. Frustrated. Could I be wrong? Then one afternoon I met with a group of evangelists for fellowship. Every one of them had a story to tell that was similar to mine. They all shared a common experience of official discouragement. They had the burning fire of the Spirit within, the challenge of vast possibilities around, but only criticism from without. Yet they refused to act, to break out of the mold.

Many times during these birth pangs I agonized in my mind and spirit. I had to spend long hours in prayer just to keep my poise and peace. *How long,* I wondered, *would it take to bring Africa to Christ without aggressive, evangelistic crusades?*

We have only one generation to save a generation. Every generation needs regeneration. Yet God's people seemed content to see millions of precious Africans die and go to hell. What tragedy. What waste. What sin.

The pressure finally reached a crisis point. One day I locked myself in a hotel room in Lesotho to pray. I determined I would not let go of God until I had a clear word from Him. I cried out to Him boldly, telling Him exactly how I felt. From my prone position on the floor, my face buried in carpet, I told Him I was sick and tired of the strain—constrained to evangelize, but restrained by men. Was this really His will for me, this constant impulse to campaign? Other workers did not seem to believe mass evangelism was a good course of action. Could I be wrong? I needed an answer.

That day God made matters clear to me. As frankly as I had spoken to the Lord, He replied: "If you drop the vision which I have given you, I shall have to look for another man who will accept it and do what I want. The choice is up to you."

With tears, I repented of my hesitations. I made my decision, forever. Then God smiled upon me. Suddenly I was filled with divine encouragement. Since that day, I have not looked back. There have been many critics, but I have learned how to handle them. I refer them to God. After all, it's His responsibility. He called me and told me what to do. Anyone who objects should take it up with the Boss, not the hired man. I have decided to concentrate on what He wants me to do rather than concentrate on the people who object to His methods. Since that time the ministry has grown—step by step, dimension to dimension, sometimes dramatically.

"Curiously Wrought"

Evangelism happens to be my calling, just as other callings grip other men and women who are apostles, pastors, teachers, prophets, elders, musicians, organizers, intercessors—workers in a thousand different capacities. Each plays an important role in the kingdom of God. None is more important than the other; all are necessary. When God puts His Hand upon us, He does two things. First, He gives us a ministry, then He opens a door to service. Each one of us has a unique and vital place in His kingdom. Every believer is individually chiseled, "curiously wrought in the lowest parts of the earth," as Psalm 139:15 puts it. All are unique. All are different. All have their place.

A new vision, however, can be disturbing. It can disturb those who receive it as well as others who do not have it. This is especially true if the new vision thrusts one man into the limelight. Sometimes this results in resentment, criticism, even jealousy. Sometimes a man's close friends have trouble believing that God could call one of their own to walk by different means and methods. But there is no accounting for God's choice, as Paul points out about Jacob. If God calls, the best proof of that call is our patience when we are misjudged and criticized. Those who know God has sent them will rest in God, and leave those who disapprove for the Lord to handle. "Humble yourselves therefore under the mighty Hand of God, that he may exalt you in due time" (1 Pet. 5:6).

One must be careful not to mishandle criticism. Sometimes, through the eyes of others, you see the back of your own head. What others say about us is important, be they enemies or friends. I praise the Lord for those choice men and women God has given me to guide me with their perception and insight. I would be a fool not to listen to them, even—and especially—when they disagree with me. Evangelists need advice. They cannot be the law to themselves. They are members of the body of Christ. And like all members, they must depend on other members. But, also, they are held solely account-able to obey the voice of God. It is a fine line to walk—but walk it they must.

Dan, the Shipowner

During the biblical period of the Judges, Israel had many ups and downs. Often the people were oppressed by invaders. When this happened God raised up charismatic leaders to unite them and to help them defend themselves. One of these judges was a woman, Deborah, who was a prophetess. In her day a Canaanite king, Jabin, sent in his men, plundering and killing under a military leader named Sisera.

Deborah felt compelled to resist. However, she was no Joan of Arc. She did not deck herself in armor to fight like a man. Instead, she used her persuasive powers to inspire the men of Israel to rally their tribes under the leadership of a young commander named Barak.

It was a critical time in the history of Israel. Deborah sent messengers to each tribe, enlisting them to unite and stand against Sisera. Some responded, some did not. In fact, viewing the reactions of the various tribes to Deborah's challenge is like holding a mirror on the church today. Deborah used the warriors from the tribes who responded and, thanks to God, wisdom and intervention won a great victory for Israel.

After it was all over, Deborah analyzed what had taken place. One of the questions she asked concerned the tribe of Dan, who had failed to respond to her call for help. Her question was, "Why did Dan remain in ships?" (Judges 5:17).

The Danites were merchants, running a kind of mercantile marine service for Israel. They brought in goods from the far corners of the earth. Then, moored in a harbor, the ships became shops, selling directly from the importer to the public.

Reading Deborah's question, I realize the same situation exists today. Dan, the businessman, was at the cash register of his shop. Business had never been better. Profits were at an all-time high. He was just closing his shop for the day when a sudden disturbance on the dock caught his attention. A messenger had arrived, exhausted from the urgent run. He was carrying an important letter to Dan. It read:

> Dear Dan,
>   Jabin, the king of Canaan, has sent Sisera to attack Israel. We are under siege and fighting with everything at our disposal. We desperately need help. The tribes must all unite to repel the enemy. Come and help—*now!* Your fellow Israelites are bleeding and dying. Please respond. Come at once!
>
>   Deborah, Judge of Israel

Dan, the businessman, was deeply moved. He jumped up and looked inland, where he thought hostilities might be in progress. He possibly heard the clash of arms and the cries of his dying brothers. But then, just as suddenly, he heard something else—the ringing of his cash register. Could he just take off and leave his money uncounted? If he went to fight, what would happen to his ships and shops? Wouldn't he be risking his flourishing enterprise? And there was something else. The Canaanites were his customers, too. Some of them actually advertised in his catalog. He must not upset them. Shouldn't he remain neutral? What if his ships sank while he was away fighting in the army?

After such considerations, he decided what he would do. Hurriedly he stuffed a bundle of money into the messenger's pockets along with a note to his old friend, Deborah:

> I certainly want to help. Regretfully, I can't come myself, but here's my contribution. Tell young Barak I'm with him in spirit.

So Dan went on counting his cash while his brethren rallied round the standard of Deborah and Barak. Let others die for Israel; Dan had a business to run. After all, if he left his store, who would finance the war? So Dan stayed safely behind, hiding in his ship—the ship of self-interest, self-love, greed, and fear.

Each of us needs to ask ourselves: *Does Dan represent me?* Dan is the Christian who belongs to the family of God, knows what the claims of

God upon him are, hears the call of God—but does not respond to it. He remains in his ship-shop when God wants him to "seek first the Kingdom of God." The music of the tinkling till, the applause of the unconverted, the risk of offending the heathen, and the opinion of family and friends deafen him to the call of the living God. In church Dan sings about "the sweet by and by . . . on that beautiful shore," but does he face the question whether his ship reaches it or forever flounders in the sea of life?

If you think such situations cannot be, just look around. See the wreckage of lives where people have chosen the wrong priorities. Some of the saddest people have been those with an eye to the main chance, who didn't keep their eyes on God.

The American poet Whittier lamented: "Of all sad words of tongue or pen, the saddest are these—'It might have been.'" These are the ones who lost their vision. They refused to risk, to dare, to follow the call of God on their lives. As a result things go terribly wrong. Success turns to ashes. Popularity goes sour. They choose the Danite opportunities of the ship-shop. They let others follow Christ to His harvest field, or battlefield, or maybe mission field. At the last they see their joy and contentment drift away and realize their own tragedy. With Jeremiah they mourn, "The harvest is past, the summer has ended, and we are not saved" (Jer. 8:20, NIV).

Makers of Money—or History?

The runner with Deborah's letter hoped for a better response when he reached the tribal areas of Zebulun and Naphtali. The two men, if I may say so, were working in the fields and in the villages under the warm sun. Younger and fitter than Dan, they were looking forward to the end of the day and to the joy of their young wives and children. They got together around the messenger to hear and consider Deborah's call to service. What should they do? To them there was only one choice—go! "Praise the Lord," they said, "that God has anointed somebody to lead us. Now, let's put an end to this constant harassment from Jabin and his bandits. Thank God for Deborah! We'll back her to the hilt. Tell her we're on the way. She can count on us."

Zebulun and Naphtali exchanged their pruning hooks for spears. Children were hugged, weeping-but-understanding wives were kissed, and the men marched away into the dust of battle. "Zebulun and Naphtali were a people that jeoparded their lives unto the death in the high places of the field" (Judg. 5:18, NIV).

The war was soon won. But it brought no glory to Dan. Deborah, a woman, had led Israel. Another woman, Jael, wife of Heber, struck the famous final blow when she pinned Sisera to the ground in her own tent with a peg through his head, ending the rampage of his Canaanite army.

Deborah then went on her judge's rounds and arrived at the harbor quay to visit Dan. She only wanted to ask him one withering question: "Why did you remain in your ship?" Dan sat still, his fingers fumbling nervously with a coin. He couldn't lift his eyes to face this Holy-Ghost-anointed woman of God. Her question would haunt him the rest of his life. Why did he stay behind and let others lead the way, when he could have responded and been one of the victors?

That question will be heard again at the throne of God, when Dan and all the rest of us have to give account for our lives. On that day will be heard "the saddest" of words: "it might have been."

Zebulun and Naphtali did not have Dan's business expertise. Dan made money; but Zebulun and Naphtali made history, fighting and winning to save Israel in a remarkable battle still talked about three thousand years later. They risked not only their businesses, but their lives, fighting in the high places of the field. Dan staked nothing. He took no risks. When he died, he was the richest—and possibly the most miserable man in Israel. He had bars of gold in his bedroom right to the ceiling. He kept his money constantly in view so he could gloat. He had lived for gold for so long he wanted to take it with him when he died. Then, as the angel of death swept him away, he heard the hollow laugh of the grim reaper, "You've made your pile, now somebody else will spend it."

The call of God is heard by the Zebuluns and Naphtalis of today, but not by the people of Dan. The Dan people are those who consider their businesses more important than God's work, their backyard gardens more important than the harvest fields, their homes more important than heaven for the lost, hoarding money more important than saving souls. "I have married a wife, and cannot come," the man in Jesus' story (Luke 14:20) replied to the call to follow God. Zebulun left his wife, though, and saved the kingdom. Any pastor knows which of his or her members represent Dan—and which represent Zebulun and Naphtali.

"It's always the same people who respond, and give, and work," pastors tell me. "If it weren't for them, this church would close." Some obey God's call at any cost, but others would not risk a dime for Him. Some of the men of Zebulun and Naphtali died on the high places of the battleground for God, but they are numbered in the Lamb's Book of Life as heroes of the faith. Others, like Dan, are listed only in the daily obituary column of the paper—tomorrow's fishwrapper.

Jesus said, "He that loseth his life . . . shall find it" (Matt. 10:39), and "Be thou faithful unto death, and I will give thee a crown of life" (Rev. 2:10). There's a nobility in that kind of dying—even in one's readiness to give all. The Lord Himself will recognize it when a glittering crown of life is placed upon one's head by the hand of Christ Himself.

Of the Dan folk, Jesus says, "He that findeth his life shall lose it" (Matt. 10: 39).

That Woman!

After the battle came the celebration. Deborah the prophetess and Barak the general sang a victory song, naming the tribes one by one. The song is full of irony. After Dan and Zebulun and Naphtali, they named Reuben, about whom it is written forever, "For the divisions of Reuben there were great searchings of heart" (Judg. 5:16).

Let me continue to draw my simple picture. The Reuben people were thoughtful types, people of consideration and judgment. They were the educated, the talkers. When the sweating and dusty messenger came panting into their midst shouting, "Urgent! Urgent! A message from Judge Deborah," Reuben quickly took the letter. Immediately he called an emergency meeting of the Council of the Wise. Together, they gave Deborah's letter the serious attention they always directed to every issue. The council members sat down and first read the minutes of the last meeting. The members then pondered the situation. They were keen thinkers. Their perceptions soon showed them it was too big a matter for any rash decision. They should not make a decision which might later be regretted. With their usual caution, it was decided they would sleep on the matter and the council would meet again the next day with fresh minds.

The next day, Deborah's call was carefully examined from every angle. The council reached a unanimous conclusion which was recorded in their minutes: Action must be taken. But before they rushed off into battle, a plan was needed. They agreed to return the next day.

The next morning a strategy was devised and general tactics were itemized. Then they discussed logistics, means, and command procedures, making wonderful progress. They adjourned for the day, but not before praying for Deborah.

The next morning the council took action which would ensure the success of the battle. They would be a first-class army. Granted, the planning was taking time, but it was better to go into battle well prepared than as a group without a plan.

During that session, they had a tea break and went out to stretch their legs, feeling content with their work thus far. While strolling, they caught the faint sound of the distant struggle and saw the smoke of burning villages in the sky. A straggler staggered into view, bleeding from his wounds. Thankfully, the council was hard at work on a project to help. Meanwhile, the battle raged—just beyond the mountains.

There was yet one major difficulty to be overcome. The council adjourned for the weekend, promising to pray for one another. They met again the following Monday to discuss the last matter on the agenda, the stickiest issue of all. Deborah! She was a woman! How could they consider the call of a mere female? Where were the scriptural grounds? When, in all history, had a woman ever taken the lead—except to lead Adam into sin? Deborah herself stood between them and action. Their learning and knowledge saw no way to permit themselves to answer her call. The action had no precedent. A female taking authority to govern and to judge? Could

God bless men who followed a woman into battle? It was sad, but clear. As godly, Bible-believing men, they had no choice but to decline. It was a matter of principle.

Sadly, the descendents of Reuben are still among us today. People often don't approve of the way things are being done. They don't approve of the leadership, or the method, or the timing, or the personnel. "We need more time to think," some say. Others counter with, "We need to train our leaders before we let them lead. That way they can be like us." Sometimes the objections are intellectual. "Evangelism? With all our education? This is not the age of Paul and Peter! Soul saving? Revivalism? That was all fine for backwoodsmen, but we need a different approach." Yet these people never find a different method. Like the Reubenites, they think themselves to death.

The Reubenites are more concerned about spirituality and quality than about plucking men from eternal burning. They make fine speeches and adorn the platform in an elegant fashion, but are never seen on the front lines. Some are ultra-devout, deeply concerned with the work of the Spirit within themselves or in their churches. An evangelist dropped in their midst would disturb and interrupt what God has been doing these past years. They can't support evangelists. Evangelists garner attention and deeper developments are hindered. So the pious words flow, and no effort is made. Precious people go on dying in their sins as the sons of Reuben continue to list their objections.

On Vacation

There is another group to discuss, the tribe of Asher. When the anxious and exhausted envoy finally reaches them, what happens? Deborah records it in her song: "Asher continued on the sea shore" (Judg. 5:17). Asher was on vacation. "I'm sorry," he told the collapsing messenger, "I need this rest. It's been more than a year since I've taken a break, and God has convicted me to take care of my body by giving it a vacation. Besides, I owe it to my wife and children."

Asher worked hard at his job. Church duties were nice for those with nothing else to do, but he had accounts to see after business hours. He often worked for weeks on end with no time off. He owed himself this break without interruption. No, he couldn't come at the moment.

"But," Asher said, "I'm sure plenty of others will turn up and help. Some people are cut out for that sort of thing. Deborah will be all right." Asher sat up in his beach chair and took a long drink. "Tell Deborah we admire her. She's marvelous. We have confidence that we can leave the matter in her hands. Whatever she does is fine with us. We'll be praying and believing for victory. Explain my predicament, that I need to stay here on the beach for a while, or I won't be any good to run my business."

The sons of Asher depend on others to do what they won't do themselves. This is all too common. "Somebody will turn up, and it will get done. It always does. I like to spend my weekends where I can get away from it all. I have a vacation place, and it would be silly not to go there." These are the ones who let any invitation take them from the cry of God. They need some relaxation at times, they rationalize, and some things *have* to be attended to. Commitment is fine for others, and they applaud them, but remember: "All work and no play makes Jack a dull boy." And that applies to God's work, too, they wisely nod.

So, what finally happens to these sons of the tribes? Dan invariably comes to his tragic end. And Reuben? I hear he dropped dead, still talking. He let Deborah down, but the undertaker was the last to let him down. As for Asher, he became overweight and his blood pressure increased because of lack of exercise. He never did a stroke, but he had one—and died. He lost his life saving it.

That is the parable from the story of Deborah. It remains a solemn matter for consideration in our own lives today. Jesus used humor when he spoke of a camel going through the eye of a needle, as he warned the rich about the difficulty they would have entering the kingdom of God. People do make excuses, like the outrageous examples Christ used in the parable of the wedding feast. One declined the invitation because he had married a wife. Another had bought land, and yet another had purchased oxen. They had their pleasures for a time—and then lost the crown forever.

Some in our own CfaN team have already received that crown. A terrible accident occurred in 1985 after we had been to a crusade in

Zaire. It was a glorious Gospel victory. As many as eighty thousand people had packed the stadium in Lubumbashi. Thousands had entered the kingdom of God when they accepted Jesus Christ as their Lord and Savior. Multitudes more had been reached through live national radio and television broadcasts.

After the crusade, our trucks were making their way back to Zambia. As they crossed the border an unknown driver in a huge tanker truck swerved into the path of one of our CfaN Gospel trucks. It was later determined the driver of the tanker had been drinking. There was a horrible head-on collision, followed by an explosion and fire. Two of our CfaN technicians, Horst Kosanke and Milton Kasselman, died in the fire as the rest of the team stood by helplessly, weeping and praying.

We were grief-stricken and shocked. Then, a great spirit of determination swept through our entire team. The work would not be stopped, not even by death and tragedy. "God buries His workers, but His work carries on."

However, everyone did not share our triumphant spirit. Back home, some people began to make negative judgments as they analyzed our mission in the spirit of Reuben. "There must be sin in the team. Stop the work. Stop the ministry. Stop the whole operation." I was amazed. If there was sin in the camp, God would not need to kill two fine men to let me know. Those pointing fingers of accusation were like Job's so-called comforters, who tried to prove his miseries were a judgment from God. These people were the sons of Reuben, sitting in their council chairs handing out judgment without cost to themselves.

I close this chapter by saying to all such Reubenites: Many are prepared to lay down their lives for Jesus in His work. Many a missionary has given his life for Africa. There are obvious dangers, and some will die—as Horst and Milton did. But thank God for men and women willing to risk it all. Others will not risk at all. CfaN team members live with Jesus closely, day by day. We are on a real battle-field with Satan, who would like to destroy us. Eighteen hundred years ago St. Tertullian wrote: "The blood of the martyrs is the seed of the church." His words have all history behind them as their proof today.

To die in the work of Christ may be God's purpose for some. Christ is glorified whether people are won for Him by our deaths or by our lives. It is all the same. I offer this as my personal challenge to all who read this book: *Be a Zebulun or a Naphtali.* Join your brothers and sisters on the battlefield! The Lord is with us. Our Captain never lost a battle. It is time to give consideration to things other than material comforts. Begin to labor for that which does not perish.

To build God's eternal kingdom means that mortal hands must do immortal work. That which is of faith in God can never die. Levi left his tax collecting. The fishermen of Bethsaida laid down their nets. The same challenge they heard and responded to is still coming to us from the living Christ. Jesus says, "Follow Me!"

4

Gasping for the Gospel

If you have ten thousand people living around your church building, four of them die every week, according to statistics. It is hardly satisfactory, then, if only one is saved every month, or even every week. The need of the Gospel is so blatant that anything I could say would be simply emphasizing the obvious. Yet I see that the devil has tricks to hide the obvious.

Satan first tried to stop the birth of the Savior. He had earlier arranged the murder of Abel and then launched hell's missiles at all Christ's human ancestors, finally slaughtering the innocents in Bethlehem. But nothing could stop the work of the Holy Spirit. The Gospel message was even more urgent on the hearts of men. Then, murder and genocide having failed, Satan realized the only alternative left was to prevent the preaching of the Gospel.

At first the devil used only persecution and false gospels. But across the years he has amassed a considerable armory. One type of weapon he uses is to give believers other priorities. He doesn't mind how hard we work for our church as long as we don't attack his evil kingdom. We can major in doctrine, in fellowship, in prosperity, or in cultivating our own soul, using ways that bear no relation to preaching the Gospel to every creature. Satan will do little to stop us. All these are good activities which nonetheless crowd out the most urgent work—winning the lost.

Satan has given us the ability to devise interpretations of the Scriptures which convince our minds and quiet our consciences about the lost. Prayer itself, while so vital, must never be substituted for evangelism. As Suzette Hattingh once said, "Prayer without evangelism is an arrow shot nowhere." If we hold prayer rallies, they should be linked to some direct evangelistic effort. To pray without acting on our prayers to win souls is totally wrong.

The world's needs are vast enough for everyone to see, and it would take a book to describe them all. If anything can help the woes of the globe, the Gospel ranks at the top of the list. To preach the Gospel is to unbind, while to withhold the Gospel is to bind. Not to preach the Gospel means we are hiding the medicine from the dying patient. This is true in Ireland, Israel, China, and Africa—just as it is in the United States and Europe. There is no hope for our world outside Jesus Christ.

Some have given up hope. They have seen the limits of science, technology, medicine, politics, and education. Cynically they turn to opiates to forget. Drugs, drink, anything—even religious mysticism. The idea that man has only man to help him is frightening. Evil grows two heads for every one that we cut off. This hydra-headed monster needs the dagger of the Cross of Christ plunged into its heart.

Every sphere of life cries out for the Gospel, like a fish gasping on the bank for water. Personally, socially, globally, religiously, the *only* hope for us is in the Gospel.

The Only New Force Available

Isaiah wrote that "your whole head is injured, your whole heart afflicted" (Isa. 1:5, NIV). Sometimes our bodies cure themselves, but often medicines are needed. These medicines reinforce the body's natural healing powers. Sickness can overcome the body's defenses, and outside help then is needed. When it comes to salvation, though, there is no other source for man except the supernatural power of the Gospel. Our task is to put that remedy on the table. Even though there are some people who will not accept it, there is no argument against the Gospel's wonderful power.

However, one never can force a cure on another, not even by threat. If the patient resolves not to take his medicine, he simply dies. The history of Israel proves that when the Jews were true to their central faith, they did well. When they handed over their hearts to others, to new religions, heathens, and super powers, disaster always followed. The spiritual life of the people of Israel was always the deciding factor in their material or political prosperity or poverty.

To treat faith in God as a secondary matter, or as a controversial side issue, is fatal. We are what we believe. All activity is regulated by faith. If we don't realize that, then we know nothing about human nature. God is the only issue that finally counts.

Fire Insurance?

What is mankind's greatest need? I learned many years ago I cannot preach the Gospel as a mere social benefit. There are social benefits once the Gospel is preached and applied, but the Gospel has to do with God. And God has to do with eternity. If you want to consider the benefits here and now, they are obvious.

- Nothing adds up without God.

- Life is meaningless without God.

- True happiness can be found only by following Jesus.

Most of us, however, realize that God has more for us than earthly happiness. He confronts us with the eternal ages. Our destiny is bound up in the Gospel. Are you saved or lost? That is the question of all questions.

The declaration of the Gospel is "Jesus saves." He saves from wrath, judgment, hell, bondage, the devil, and darkness. He saves us from dying in our sins. Sure, there are some who scorn the Gospel as mere "fire insurance." Well, what is wrong with fire insurance? It is a crazy householder who is not insured. We know, though, that salvation is far more. And who else offers such insurance but Jesus?

Why Humanity Suffers

For years I pondered the question, Why does God allow so much suffering in the world? Then I realized to ask that question was tantamount to asking the government's secretary of transportation why he or she allows so many accidents on the roads. The secretary would point to the book of traffic laws and reply, "Every time a law is broken, an accident and suffering might occur."

People suffer chiefly for one reason—they are ignoring God's book, the Bible. When they ignore it, when they break its "rules," things go wrong. That's not God's fault. Our Creator knows how He made us. Consequently He says, "Thou shalt not" do certain things. God doesn't say this to spoil our fun, but because God knows that our psyche cannot handle sin and actually is crushed by misdeeds.

It is always wise to read the instruction manual before using a new appliance. People are worried about breaking a tape recorder or a washing machine, but don't seem to mind destroying their own spirits and souls with the poison of sin. The need to preach the Gospel is desperate!

The Meaning of the Cross

Is the Gospel a call to discipleship? The question is debated. One matter is sure—Jesus asks no one to take up *their* cross until they have found salvation and strength at *His* Cross. We are not saved by denying ourselves and carrying our own cross. We are saved by the redeeming power of the atoning death of Jesus Christ. We trust many will become disciples and take up their crosses, of course, but first they must kneel at His Cross.

That Cross of Jesus consists of two beams: one vertical and one horizontal. Those crossed timbers are twin symbols of human misery and God's salvation. The horizontal beam is like a dash, the very sign used for a minus. That is the human story. We were born with a minus, a deficit, a void. Something is missing, but people are at a complete loss to know what it is. They talk about their search for truth, but they don't even know what they mean by truth. They are like Pontius Pilate who, standing before Jesus, stumbled over *the* Truth asking, "What is truth?" That is man's minus outlook.

Jesus came, though. Outside Jerusalem, on a low hill, a vertical timber was raised which crossed through our minus sign. Jesus hung there on that upright, and He thus turned our minus into a *plus.* The Romans thought the cross was just an instrument of execution, but it was God's plus sign for minus-minded mankind.

Indeed, give the Cross a second look, and it is even more than a plus—it is a multiplication sign. "I am come that they might have life, and that they might have it more *abundantly*" (John 10:10). The apostle Peter wrote, "May grace and peace be *multiplied* to you" (1 Pet. 1:2, RSV). Abundance is at the very heart of the Gospel.

That is why we must preach this glorious Gospel. Think of the many reversals the Savior causes. Jesus Christ turns loss into gain, negatives into positives, night into light, hate into love, bondage into freedom, failure into success, sickness into health, weakness into strength, evil into righteousness, and more—so much more. What a Gospel! Praise be to God! Nothing in all human knowledge can compete with that dazzling splendor. It is the greatest work on earth to preach the good news, and the need for the Gospel is the greatest need in the world.

In a British city where I preached, someone told me that contractors had built a mosque. As is customary they returned six months later to correct any flaws which may have developed. One door was sticking, and they sent a workman to fix it. But the Muslim leader refused the repair, explaining that if the door was like that, it was the will of Allah and must remain as it was.

Jesus leaves nothing sticking and wrong. If it needs changing, He can and will change it. His will is never faulty. The purpose of the Gospel is to change a whole world which is wrong. Hallelujah!

The Prodigal Planet

If the subject of eternal life does not show the *urgency* of proclaiming the Gospel to every creature, I cannot think of anything else that will. True, other faiths are out there. But anyone who surveys them will know they are totally empty of any Gospel promise. The Eastern mind cults could offer only transient benefits, even if they did work. But the Gospel does not have merely mental poise in view. The efforts that the cults insist must be made to achieve harmony with nature are not worthwhile. Jesus did not come to give us religious feelings or to suggest a system of mind power. He came to *save us*, not to explain how our "inner resources" can be tapped to save ourselves. Jesus was not a teacher of transcendental meditation, or quietism, or yoga, or stoicism. He was and is, first and foremost, a Savior.

As for other religions, which of them offers eternal life *now?* Some only promise the end of existence. Karma teachings see life as such a misery that obliteration is the only way out! Buddha equated life as nirvana—an existence without meaning or purpose. Then there is the paradise promise, which consists of endless sensual pleasure. That sounds more like hell than heaven to me.

The supreme wonder of the Gospel is its present realization of life—life of such quality that it cannot fade for eternity. Speaking to the sister of Lazarus as she stood mourning outside his tomb, Jesus said,

"I am the resurrection, and the life: he that believeth in me, though he were dead, yet shall he live:
And whosoever liveth and believeth in me shall never die.
Believest thou this?" (John 11:25–26)

That's real life! And best of all, it is available to us *now!* Urgent? The world gasps for the Gospel like a fish out of water. That is the number-one reason for preaching the Gospel. To preach it for any other reason than to see souls saved means you don't understand the reason for the Gospel to begin with. I have heard of ministers who have preached for years and have never seen anyone saved. Others have told me they literally have no desire to see souls saved from their preaching. Unbelievable! There is no other reason to preach the Gospel than to see men saved from hell and enter the kingdom of heaven.

The present world desperately needs the Gospel! When we go God's way, the world is ours. When we resist Him, we resist His own concern for us. We spoil His plans to bless us, and happiness is destroyed. We have gotten to the stage today where we are brilliant at destruction, from the ruin of graffiti upon walls to the threat of the obliteration of the entire environment. We war, we hate, we trample on the fair earth and foul all that He gives us.

Most of this destruction comes from sheer evil, or else from selfish greed. Basically, it comes from our turning away from God. Most of man's ills are manmade. The Gospel reverses these fatal processes. It brings us back to do His will, and His will is always for the good of us all. God loves His prodigal planet, and if we return we shall "begin to be merry," and enjoy the welcome of the Father.

I Have Seen It Happen!

God is sweeping some parts of the world with the Gospel. The outcome is salvation: sins forgiven, races living in harmony, crime cured, stolen property returned by the truckload, marriages restored, families reunited, evil men turned into saints, death-dealing addictions cured and illness miraculously healed. The Gospel is the most elevating force on earth. It has not come to level us all to the lowest common denominator, but to create new lives, and to give to all the dignity of the sons of God! Men who once were savages are reclaimed to walk as princes. Hallelujah!

What a reason to preach the Gospel! Could anything be more thrilling, adventurous, and worthwhile? What else is worth life's effort? The salvation of the world? Well, Jesus did not think it a waste of time to go out of His way to heal the sick and feed the feckless multitudes. He invited persecution for healing a man with a withered arm, and from that moment on He walked with a price on His head. That man mattered to Jesus, and his arm had to be restored, no matter what (Matt. 12:10). People who believe in the Gospel also believe in caring for the physical needs of people. The less we believe in God, the less we value mankind. Atheism bred Adolf Hitler and Joseph Stalin. Atheism erased millions as if they were no more than figures in chalk on a child's blackboard! Preaching the Gospel is part of God's plan to put us, as it were, back in Eden.

Nonetheless, suppose the impossible—that science and politics could put us back in the Garden of Eden. Wouldn't our restlessness reduce it once again to ruin? There is one reason we desire Eden, though many do not realize it. Men and women want those conditions again in which they heard the voice of God in the garden. We don't yearn for Utopia. We yearn for the presence of God.

Some churchmen say that "man is a social animal," as if the herd instinct is all that is worth mentioning about that marvelous creation called man. We are more than a herd—we are each made for God, and nothing but a relationship with Him will ever content us.

Sometimes when inspired music touches us, we get a sense of infinity. Music only points to it, though. The music echoes a faraway greatness that it cannot fulfill. That infinity is God Himself, and what music only suggests is given to us when we receive salvation through Jesus Christ and begin to worship Him.

God is our natural habitat. Until we find Him, as we do when we obey the Gospel, we are caged. Men everywhere are beating themselves against the bars of their own materialism and unbelief. Their very money becomes their prison. Deep calls to deep, and height to height within our souls. Our art, our poetry, our works of beauty are the expressions of imprisoned creatures who remember the glories of the free air and the mountains. While good in themselves, these expressions remain mere reflections of reality until a soul comes into salvation. Jesus is the reality behind all we see or do, and the Gospel releases us from bondage, allowing us to come into our true element.

Somebody said that "Christians are happy in their way." In their way? In what sort of way are unbelievers happy? In no sort of way, I think. Christians are happy in God's way, the originally intended way. The God scene is the only scene. Outside are the wastes of the wilderness and the horizons where dawn never breaks, where the godless will never be happy in any way. Unbelievers will have to extract what drink they can from the dry ground of resentment, doubt, and hatred. But the Spirit and the Bride say, "Come . . . and drink from the fountain of life freely." A way of life is preached in the Gospel that leads more and more unto the perfect day. That is another reason for the Gospel to be preached. There can be no greater urgency!

Part Two
The Gospel

5
God's New Elishas

Christ's Great Commission is not a scrap of paper, blown to our feet by the winds of history from twenty centuries ago. It is Jesus, standing in the midst of His church today, saying, "Go ye. . . . for I am with you."

Suppose Jesus were to come into your room one night, stand at the foot of your bed, and shake you awake. Then, once He had your attention, suppose He were to say to you personally, "I have something I want you to do. Go into all the world and preach the Gospel to every creature."

Would you do as He asked?

Imagine that you had a vision of the Lord in your church, like the one John had on Patmos. Suppose He appeared in your pulpit one Sunday and spoke to everybody, saying, "Go ye into all the world and preach the Gospel to every creature, and signs shall follow them that believe."

What would you do? Would you shake His hand at the door after the service and murmur, "Fine sermon today, Jesus!" Would you carry on just the same as usual, forgetting the words of the sermon before you opened the door of your car to drive home? Or would you press on more urgently to witness for Christ?

If anyone wonders whether the Great Commission is relevant today, they may as well ask if plowing and harvesting are relevant. Or if getting out of bed is! "Relevant" is not the word. The word is urgent. The Gospel is our existence.

A Christian is a witness. The name "Christian" was coined in early Antioch because it easily identified believers. They were the people who always talked about Christ. The Christian's business is not busy-ness, but witnessing. Witnessing is the commerce of the people of the kingdom of God.

The written commands of Christ in Scripture are just as immediate as if He spoke to us personally in a vision. The Great Commission is "our baby." Our work in this task is not optional. The Lord does not ask, "Would you mind helping Me? I would like to invite you."

He says: "Ye have not chosen me, but I have chosen you, and ordained you, that ye should go and bring forth fruit, and that your fruit should remain" (John 15:16).

In that statement He was not talking about election to salvation, but rather of election to service. We do not serve at *our* discretion. The Great Commission is like a military draft "call-up," not a suggestion for our consideration. We are not to go for the sake of going, but because we are sent by Jesus.

In fact, Christ's command is much more than that. Jesus turns us into witnesses. He changes our nature by His Spirit within us. He did not tell us, "Witness!" He said, "Be witnesses!" It was a creative word. God said, "Let there be light," and light broke in upon us. Jesus chose us and then made us light bearers.

"For we are his workmanship, created in Christ Jesus unto good works" (Eph. 2:10). These good works are to "shew the exceeding riches of his grace" (v. 7). If we did not show the world the riches of His grace, it would be foreign to our new nature in Christ. What the Holy Spirit has planted within us is the Spirit of witness. But we can become slack and let the light within us die down through neglect. Fruitless branches are pruned. Now we have a wonderful guarantee. When we go as He says, He goes with us.

Suppose we do not comply? Is He still with us? Well, one thing is sure. The anointing of the Spirit only comes with obedience. The anointing and the Great Commission go together.

Transferred Mandate

Here is a word from the Lord for us today. His Voice came to me from a corner of the Bible not always noticed:

And the Lord said unto him [Elijah], Go, return on thy way to the wilderness of Damascus: and . . . anoint Hazael to be king over Syria.

And Jehu the son of Nimshi shalt thou anoint to be king over Israel: and Elisha the son of Shaphat of Abel–meholah shalt thou anoint to be prophet in thy room.(1 Kings 19:15–16)

Three men had to be anointed—Hazael, Jehu, and Elisha. That is not so remarkable. However, what actually happened is another matter. Elijah failed to carry out two-thirds of God's command. He never anointed Hazael or Jehu. In fact, there is no record he actually anointed Elisha, either. But Elijah did go and find Elisha. At Elijah's death, Elisha's request came to pass: A double portion of Elijah's mantle, or anointing, rested on Elisha. Elisha thus received a "double portion" of Elijah's spirit. That is, the same Spirit that had anointed Elijah then anointed Elisha to carry out the same commission. Later, it was Elisha who anointed Hazael and Jehu.

Notice: Elijah's commission, with Elijah's power, was transmitted to Elisha. A dual transfer took place, from the prophet who was leaving to the prophet who was staying. God's commission and authority remained when Elijah left, falling upon Elisha. In short, the mandate was transferable.

That is a divine principle. God's call and His power are transferable. The Great Commission and the promises that go with it made the disciples what they eventually would become. The same commission and the same promises were passed on to us, in order that we could do and be what the first disciples did and were. We are the heirs of the apostles.

It goes without saying that the commission of Christ to us is far more important than Elijah's commission. And the promised anointing is even greater. Read it again:

Go ye therefore and teach all nations, baptizing them in the name of the Father, and of the Son, and of the Holy Ghost:

Teaching them to observe all things whatsoever I commanded you: and, lo, I am with you alway, even unto the end of the world. Amen. (Matt. 28:19–20)

While the King James Version of that verse reads, "even unto the end of the world," the New King James Version translates it, "to the end of the age." That means now, tomorrow, and beyond. In other words, if Jesus did appear and speak to us today, He would say the same thing today He said then. He has not changed.

People want to know what the Lord is saying to the church today. He, no doubt, has many things to say, just as He did in the "letters of Jesus" in chapters two and three of the Book of Revelation. But if we are not busy doing what He already has told us to do, He will only have one thing to say: "Get on with it!"

There is no need to wait for another letter when you have not opened the first one yet. Jesus has no further word for us until His standing orders are carried out.

Many are waiting for God to speak, but only if He says what they want Him to say. They wait and wait for God to give them a new direction. But how do they know He *has* a new direction for them? Or that He has a new revelation? Or that He will give them radical instructions? The word I have from God is that He wants the old direction—a witnessing church, where evangelism is central. Until this major command is put into effect, everything else is irrelevant.

On my part, I believe we should have a humble attitude and pray that the mantle of earlier men and women of God will rest upon us. There would be no church of today had it not been for their power in revival. Many of them were true Elijahs. They took up the Great Commission and became God's brightest luminaries.

John had the mind of Jesus when he wrote, "I write no new commandment unto you, but an old commandment which ye had from the beginning" (1 John 2:7). Jesus doesn't keep on issuing fresh legislation like today's governments, which make treaties and break them, and issue new laws that are wiped from the book when the next government comes into power. What He once said, He has said once and for all. His Word remains His will! There are no hidden secrets for superior saints. His instruction is simple: "Go!"

The newspapers recently reported that a London motorist, entering the city during the early-morning rush hour, was half asleep as he waited at a traffic light. When the light changed from red to green he just sat there, staring through the windshield. An irritated driver behind him, already late for work, jumped out of his car and came around to the snoozing driver's window. "That light says, 'Go!'" he screamed. "What are you waiting for, personal permission from the minister of transportation?"

The church has a green light—*and* a personal invitation—from God. We cannot afford to sit there, asleep at the wheel. It's time to go!

No Hand-Me-Downs

Although Elisha inherited Elijah's commission, there is no record of Elijah ever instructing Elisha to go and anoint Hazael and Jehu. That instruction must have come from God through personal revelation—giving Elisha the same command He had earlier given Elijah. Even though we are linked up with generations of God's people before us, the Great Commission is transferred to us not by others but by the Lord Himself. God always operates with originals. His mandate is direct, not by tradition.

"How shall they preach, except they be sent?" Paul asked in Romans 10:15. The Spirit says the same thing as He sends us into the world. The Holy Spirit is the Spirit of witness. Witness is His purpose. The Great Commission is inseparably linked to the Holy Spirit. When Christ baptizes us into the Spirit, He puts into our hands His instructions to take the Gospel to the whole world.

Everything comes from the Master Himself—not in a general way, but in an individual way. We don't need to go to men for their power. Each of us can find all the power we need through our own Holy-Spirit baptism—direct from the Lord. We are not called by the will of men, but by the will of God. Paul begins seven of his epistles with just that emphasis.

Along with the call comes the directive to encourage others to also receive the Holy Spirit. I often put my hands on men and women, praying that Jesus will baptize them in the Holy Spirit and use them in evangelism. But we must always remember, it is Jesus alone who baptizes. Jesus told His disciples, "*I* . . . have ordained you" (John 15:16, emphasis added).

If the anointing of the Holy Spirit could have been transferred only by the early apostles, the church would have died at the end of the first century. Instead, fresh oil is available from the Lord for each generation. The wise virgins in Jesus' parable did not and could not share their oil with those whose lamps had run dry (Matt. 25:8–9). Each of us must have our own oil, direct from Jesus.

The Package Deal

The Great Commission to the disciples is transferred to each one of us individually today. Along with it comes the individual anointing of the Holy Spirit. The command and the power are one package deal. Jesus told His disciples to tarry in Jerusalem until they were endued with power. Then, He said, they would be witnesses in all the world. If you separate the commission from the enabling, you have either power without purpose or purpose without power. Power tools come with the job. If you try to get the job done with your own rusty hand wrench, you will make little progress.

One with the Apostles

The same endowment that Elisha received from Elijah was also given to John the Baptist many years later. Luke says John the Baptist came in "the spirit and power of Elijah" (Luke 1:17, NIV). The same Spirit that made Elijah—and Elisha—great prophets, was passed on also to John, whom Jesus called the greatest "that are born of women" (Matt. 11:11).

But it did not end with John. That same Spirit was upon the apostles. It also rested upon the martyrs and the confessors, as well as on those who followed. Has that Spirit now vanished? No! The thrilling truth is that the Spirit who made them all one with Elijah makes us one with them all. He is still here. We can include ourselves in His company. The Spirit of Elijah, Elisha, John, the apostles, and the early church leaders has never left. He has been among men from generation to generation. That Spirit is our inheritance. We were born to belong to His company.

We are on God's revival team, right alongside Whitfield, Wesley, Finney, Evans, Wigglesworth, Moody, Price, and Jeffreys. We share the platform, hand in hand with all God's anointed ones. We—yes, *we*—come in the Holy Spirit—in the spirit and the power of Elijah. What belonged to the great men of God is ours today, and what is ours was once theirs. The Holy Spirit is the Spirit of the prophets, poured out upon all flesh today.

These believers were all Elijahs, just as we now are Elishas. What they did, we shall do. Jesus said, "Other men laboured, and ye are entered into their labours" (John 4:38). We identify with them all. They brought the flame of Pentecost to us right from the upper room in Jerusalem. Now we carry it further. What inspired them inspires us: the same Gospel, the same Book, the same love, the same Christ of Calvary, and the same Holy Spirit.

The men of the historic revivals have gone. All have left. Only the One who met Saul on the Damascus Road and Peter in Galilee remains. He is with us! He still is baptizing into the Holy Spirit.

With that anointing, however, often come the same persecutions. The Great Commission, the anointing of the Holy Spirit, and the opposition go together. As always, the followers of Jesus will be defamed and mocked by the worldly wise. They will consider you, a believer, to be out of touch if you do not follow them in their unbelief and rationalism. These who expound this rationalism begin with a nonmiraculous creed, and then take the scissors to Scripture to make it fit.

If we share Christ's work, we share in His suffering. But "if we suffer we shall also reign with him" (2 Tim. 2:12). When people say the same things about you as they said about God's people in the past, rejoice that you are identified with them! Whoever treats you today as the New Testament people were treated nearly two thousand years ago proves that you belong to that glorious New Testament company. When you carry out the same Commission they did, with the same authority, you also will have the same enemies. Whenever the devil treats you as his foe, rejoice! He is paying you the best compliment possible. He is ranking you with those he hated in the past, the beloved servants of the most high God.

David Livingstone's Prophecy

In 1986 we had one of our huge Gospel crusades in Blantyre, Malawi, East Africa. Blantyre is named after the town in Scotland where the great missionary David Livingstone was born. Livingstone had planted a Christian mission in the area and had founded a city that now has 300,000 inhabitants, making it the largest city in Malawi today.

In his diary Livingstone wrote:

> We are like voices crying in the wilderness; we prepare the way for a glorious future. Future missionaries will be rewarded with conversions for every sermon. We are their pioneers and helpers.
>
> Let them not forget the watchmen of the night—us, who worked when all was gloom, and no evidence of success in the way of conversion cheered our paths. They will doubtlessly have more light than we; but we can serve our Master earnestly and proclaim the Gospel as they will do.

When Livingstone died in 1873, his body was returned to Scotland, but his heart was removed and buried in Africa by those he loved. Now we were there in Blantyre—more than one hundred years later. What about Livingstone's prophetic words? Were they merely wishful thinking? I rejoice to tell you what we saw. The seed sown so long ago now is blooming into harvest. In one meeting alone we saw 150,000 gathered to hear the Gospel. The people of Malawi heard about the same God as Livingstone's, the same Savior as Paul's, the same Gospel as Peter's. We were there sixteen days, and tens of thousands responded to Livingstone's message as we preached it for him and for Jesus. It reverberated throughout the whole country. The Holy Spirit spoke to my heart and said, "You are walking on the tears of former generations." Suddenly I saw it all. We were linked up with God in a movement that included His earlier workers, too, and so we were one with them all. We belonged to their team, to their mission. We were reaping with joy what they had sown in tears before us.

We do not have this harvest because we are superior to those precious men and women, but only because the harvest season has arrived. Both those who have sown and those who reap will receive the reward, according to the Word of the Lord of the harvest.

> He that reapeth receiveth wages, and gathereth fruit unto life eternal; that both he that soweth and he that reapeth may rejoice together. I sent you to reap that whereon ye bestowed no labour; other men laboured, and ye entered into their labours. (John 4:36, 38)

This is harvest time—believe it! The world's multitudes have multiplied. The opportunity is vast, exciting. And we—you and all of us—are the privileged ones chosen to do the reaping.

Knowing that so much already was done long before we ever arrived on the scene should keep us humble in times of success. We are trusted not to fail the sowers. We owe it to them to get out the sickle, or, better still, to use a combine harvester!

The Elijahs, the Pauls, the Justin Martyrs, the Livingstones—all relied on us for the future. They expected us to take advantage of all their labors. We cannot be proud—only privileged!

A Remarkable Meeting

In 1961, at twenty-one years of age, I completed my Bible college studies in the United Kingdom. Returning to my home in northern Germany, my route took me through London. My train was not due to leave until the evening, so I had time to do some sightseeing. I just walked as my feet took me, without a plan. For some reason I wandered south of the River Thames into the pleasant avenues of Clapham.

There, at a certain corner, behind a high wooden fence, I saw a name on a panel—"George Jeffreys." I had just read a book by this evangelist, and could hardly imagine that I had chanced upon the very house where that same man might be. George Jeffreys was part of the Welsh revival, and with his brother Stephen and other members of the Jeffreys family, had introduced the Full-Gospel message publicly to the people of Britain. His work shook cities. Tens of thousands witnessed mighty miracles. Eagerly I ventured through the gate and up the path to ring the doorbell.

A lady appeared at the door. "Is this the George Jeffreys, whom God used so mightily?" I asked. She affirmed it was so, to my great delight. I then asked hopefully, "Could I please see Mr. Jeffreys?"

Her reply was firm. "No, that is not possible."

Then that deep, musical Welsh voice that was said to have held thousands spellbound with its authority, spoke from inside. "Let the young man come in."

Thrilled, I entered, and there he was. He was seventy-two, but looked to me like a man of ninety.

"What do you want?" he asked.

I introduced myself, and we talked about the work of God. Suddenly the great man fell on his knees, pulling me down beside him. He started to bless me. Then the power of the Holy Spirit entered the room. The anointing began to flow. Like Aaron's oil, it seemed to run over my head and "down to the skirts of my robes."

I left that house dazed. Fours week later George Jeffreys was translated to glory. I had been led to see him just before he died. But I knew that I had picked up something from this Holy-Ghost, fire-brand evangelist. The Lord, I am sure, had arranged that meeting. How else would it have been possible for me to stumble upon this one house in a city of ten million people when George Jeffreys was not even on my mind? Whatever this experience did for me, one thing I can claim. Seeing this man of God made me understand that we build on the people who have gone before us. The city of God is built on the foundations of the apostles.

I liken it to a relay race. One man runs with a baton, another man grabs it and runs, then another, and another. They all share in the race and in the victory. If one drops the baton, or even runs a little badly, the efforts of all the rest are spoiled, and the whole team loses.

The book of Hebrews speaks of a "cloud of witnesses." They stand looking over the battlements of glory, cheering us on. We are running for them. We must do a little more than they did, not a little less. This is the last lap before Jesus comes. We cannot rest on *their* laurels. The finish line is in sight. "And this gospel of the kingdom shall be preached in all the world for a witness unto all nations; and then shall the end come" (Matt. 24:14).

God's theme for this hour is *Evangelism by Fire*. It is evangelism by the gifts, the power, and the manifestation of the Holy Spirit. Pentecost is revival!

Let me ask you a personal question. Do you find it hard to win souls for Jesus, and so you have stopped trying? Since God's primary message to all believers is to be witnesses, shouldn't that problem be first on your agenda? Shouldn't it be first on any church agenda? Surely you're not holding back because the times are difficult. Or are you? Dr. David H. C. Read writes about a young minister in a tough area of New York, who poured out his woes to a local policeman. The officer tried to cheer him up by saying, "The fact is, Reverend, this is not the kind of district for a Christian church."

The minister went home and began to think about what the cop had said. Suddenly he came alive. Where else should a Christian church be except in the midst of problem areas? What else is a Christian church supposed to be doing, if not operating where the need is greatest?

Doubters like to be clever. They analyze the situation and point out the impossibilities with high-flown language. They "prove" that nothing can be done, using words like pluralism, hedonism, insularism, and narcissism. They show with high-sounding terms that the situation is hopeless. Some areas of life, they say, are impossible even for God.

The doubters are wrong. This is God's reaping time, and He has prepared for everything. Something *can* be done. Remember: It is not by might, nor by power, but by God's Spirit that mountains are removed. We are not to rely on television, radio, money, or education—as good as these things may be. The miracle power of Jesus is all we need. When it is seen, the media will beat a path to our door.

We have only one generation to reach this generation. The original Gospel mandate is impossible without the original power. The perfect strategy of God is complete. He included you in it, and He included me in it. We are woven into and enmeshed in His plans, plans that cannot fail. If we know that, then we can do it . . . weather it . . . finish it . . . no matter what.

6

The Matchless Message

Don't argue—shine! You can't conquer darkness by arguing with it. Just switch the light on. The Gospel is power. Power creates light. When you are plugged in the light comes on.

God's power lines draw current from Calvary, the Resurrection, and from the throne of God Himself. This is what Paul had in mind when he wrote that the Gospel "is the power of God" (Rom. 1:16). He knew. He had proven it. The world in Paul's day could not have been worse. It was cruel, corrupt, and cynical. Yet the Gospel changed it. The Gospel can do it again.

Letting Loose the Power Gospel

One preacher told me he was afraid of the raw power of the Gospel—afraid to turn it loose on his people for fear it would "overcharge" them. What he needed, he told me, was a transformer to reduce the emotional appeal of the Gospel. He wanted to tone down the voltage from high to low.

Converting sinners, however, requires full Gospel power. When I preach I don't fiddle around with a low-power 12-volt system. I preach at 220 volts and pray the Lord will increase the power. I preach to convict and convert. My job is not to entertain, not to make people smile and go home feeling cozy. The salvation message, while good news, is not soothing syrup. It is a shocking message, designed to jolt men from the lethargy of their sin and tradition and electrify them into the light. I come to *save* souls, not to stroke them! Smiling happiness will follow.

I love to read the story in Acts 8 of Philip, the evangelist, meeting the Ethiopian official. The Ethiopian was the queen's financial chief, a man of business, with no time for small talk. Once Philip was invited into his chariot he didn't bother to ask what the man's needs were in order to start counseling him for hours. Philip knew the man's need. The Ethiopian, although a high official, needed Christ. Salvation is everyone's need. Philip got right down to essentials. He "preached unto him Jesus" (Acts 8:35).

Jesus is the beginning and the end of every Gospel sermon, the alpha and the omega of all witness. We are not doctrine mongers. We are not religion pushers. We are not enthusiasts. We are witnesses to Christ. He is the be-all and the end-all of the message.

What did Jesus preach? He talked about Himself. Walking on the Emmaus road with Cleopas and a friend, He explained to them, going throughout the Scriptures, the "things concerning himself" (Luke 24:27).

All His teaching goes back to Himself. For example, the day He began His public ministry, He returned to Nazareth and went into the synagogue. For twenty years He had attended that same synagogue every week. The custom was to allow men who were known to read the Scriptures, and perhaps comment on them afterward. Naturally, when He was present at the synagogue, He was invited to do this. He went forward, picked up the scroll containing the prophets, and read from the Book of Isaiah:

> The Spirit of the Lord is upon me, because he hath anointed me to preach the Gospel to the poor; he hath sent me to heal the brokenhearted, to preach deliverance to the captives, and recovering of sight to the blind, to set at liberty them that are bruised,
> To preach the acceptable year of the Lord. (Luke 4:18–19)

Nobody in the synagogue thought much of that. Most knew the words by heart. They were words that dated back eight hundred years and had been read time and time again in that same synagogue. Jesus then handed the scroll back to the synagogue leader.

He took it with great reverence, kissed it, and put it away—to be forgotten until next week. But, suddenly, that scroll seemed to become a stick of dynamite. The Word on the lips of Jesus produced an explosive effect all right. The drowsy congregation came to life—as though someone had plugged each one of them into a high-voltage circuit.

The Acceptable Year

There are seven distinct statements in the verses Jesus read, and they all apply to who He is—*today*.

He said, "This day is this Scripture fulfilled in your ears" (v.21). He declared Himself to be the Anointed One, the Christ, the One destined by the Father to perform all those promised exploits.

The first six statements can be summed up in the last one, "to preach the acceptable year of the Lord." That "acceptable year" is actually the Jubilee year. The Jubilee (jubile in the King James Version) was instituted by God to give everybody a holiday for a year. It was a year when all bond servants were to be set free, all debts were to be canceled, all mortgages returned to the owners.

Unfortunately, as we read the historical story in the Bible, it appears the Jubilee trumpet was never blown. The nation never took its sabbatical year—a failure which God held against them. The Lord would have been delighted with such gladness. God's style is to promote happiness; He loves celebrations. Even though the nation did not celebrate the Jubilee year, God meant for them to have it, and would provide it for them in a far greater way than the Jubilee of Moses described in Leviticus 25:

> Thou shalt cause the trumpet of the jubilee to sound on the tenth day of the seventh month. . . . And ye shall hallow the fiftieth year, and proclaim liberty throughout all the land unto all the inhabitants thereof: it shall be a *jubile* unto you . . . . Ye shall not therefore oppress one another . . . for I am the Lord your God. (vv. 9–10, 17, emphasis added)

The leaders were told to "proclaim liberty"! That word is still being commanded by God. We are not to preach for effects, for pulpit display, or to charm, excite, or scare folk. We are not to preach to calm people down. We are to do what Jesus did in the synagogue in Nazareth: announce liberty. That day the real Jubilee began. It was a time of deliverance, of salvation. It was to be a Jubilee, not merely for Israel, but for the whole world. A Jubilee for the foreigners He mentioned—Naaman, the Syrian leper, and the Lebanese widow of Zarephath.

The synagogue congregation marveled at this new teaching but were lost in this unfamiliar landscape of Christ's prospects for the entire world. The world He loved was too big for them. Their fears were roused. His words ignited murderous passions, feelings that were never too far below the surface in those days. Jesus' sermon certainly produced a response—the members of the congregation dragged Him from the synagogue and attempted to throw Him over a precipice!

Yet the content of His message was wonderful: freedom, deliverance, healing, and no debts! But, whatever the reaction, Jesus preached His Gospel.

So must we.

Debt in those days was tragic. Parents and their families became slaves and could never get free. Only the Jubilee could release them. Then the debtors could go home. The law said "Go!" Following the Jubilee, any slave would be a slave by his own choice.

Jesus Christ has proclaimed the Jubilee for the whole human race. All Israel knew about the Jubilee, and they knew virtually nothing. Since it had never been practiced, it now became only a poor image of the real Jubilee of the kingdom of God. Lives set free, sins' debt wiped out, deliverance for body, spirit, and soul. There are no sweating slaves in that kingdom. No fetters. Nobody is devil-driven. Hallelujah! What a Jubilee!

Isaiah describes it:

> To give unto them beauty for ashes, the oil of joy for mourning, the garment of praise for the spirit of heaviness. . . . They shall build the old wastes, they shall raise up the former desolations, and they shall repair the waste cities. . . . Ye shall eat the riches of the Gentiles. . . .

Everlasting joy shall be upon them. . . . Thou shalt no more be termed Forsaken. . . . Salvation cometh. . . . And they shall call them . . . The redeemed of the Lord. (61:3–4, 6–7; 62:4, 11–12)

In Nazareth, the Lord turned these old scriptures into a royal proclamation of a new dispensation. He announced an amnesty for all prisoners of the devil—"He led captivity captive" (Eph. 4:8).

"Sin shall not have dominion over you," the Bible says in Romans 6:14. Paul writes in Galatians that, "When the fulness of the time was come, God sent forth his Son . . . To redeem them that were under the law" (4:4–5).

The Jubilee Is Now

This is "the acceptable year of the Lord." High technology has not made deliverance unnecessary. In every nation the enslaved abound: slaves to every contemptible habit, to fear, to doubt, to depression. The devil never lets anyone out on parole. Everywhere people are failure-prone, sin-prone, morally defective, spiritually in chains. How ridiculous! Why? Because the Jubilee trumpet has sounded. We have been set free. All we have to do is accept our wonderful liberty.

That's why I tell everyone: Preach it! People have forgotten it, forgotten that Christ has set us free and is still setting men free. This is not the pre-Christian era. We are not waiting, as are the Orthodox Jews, for Christ to come and conquer. The war is over. Freedom is ours. Jesus opened the kingdom of liberty and blew the trumpet of emancipation when He cried on the cross, *"It is finished!"*

People who should know better are calling this the "post-Christian" era—as if the work of Christ was only for a past age! That simply is not true. Christ opened prison doors forever, not just for a certain period in the past. The work of Jesus cannot be exhausted or undone. It is the greatest redemptive force at work on earth today. Never again can prison doors be bolted on human beings. When Jesus opens a door, no man can shut it. "If the Son sets you free, you will be free indeed" (John 8:36, NIV). Why do millions languish in the devil's concentration camp? Today is the day of amnesty. The Conqueror has crashed through the gates—relief has arrived.

The most famous escaper of all time was Houdini, a show-business magician. Police would lock him up in a cell and, as they walked away, he would follow them—already loose within seconds. Except once. Half an hour went by and Houdini still was fuming over the lock. Then a policeman came and simply pushed the door open. The door had never been locked! Houdini was fooled by a door that was already unlocked.

Christ has gone right through the castle of giant despair. He has the keys of death and hell. He has opened the gates. So why are millions sweating, trying every trick to get out of their evil habits and bondages? They join new cults or old heathen religions, hear new theories, go to psychiatrists. Why? Jesus has already set them free. All they need to do is push open the door and accept Him.

That's the Gospel! You don't preach *about* it, you preach *it*. You don't offer its contents for discussion. The Gospel is not a discussion point. It is a proclamation of deliverance.

Dialogue? The Gospel is not open to modification. It is mandatory, a royal and divine edict. Some systems and theories of deliverance are bondages in themselves, full of lifelong duties and demands. Only Jesus saves.

A man once told me that he was a "spiritual counselor." However, he didn't believe that Jesus Christ was the Son of God, nor that the Bible was the Word of God. I wondered, therefore, how this "counselor" counseled anybody.

"Do they come to you and then go away with broken hearts?" I asked.

"Oh, no," he assured me, "I just calm them down."

I looked him in the eye and said, "Mister, a man on a sinking ship needs more than a tranquilizer. He needs the ability to walk on water—or at least enough sense to get into a lifeboat. Don't calm him down. He is going down already—down with the sinking ship. When Jesus comes to a man in a shipwreck, He doesn't throw him a Valium tablet and say, 'Perish in peace.' He reaches down His nail-scarred hand, grips him, lifts him, and says to him, 'I live and you shall live also.'"

This is the Gospel of Jesus Christ that *must* be preached: *Jesus is the Savior of our world.* This message is life, peace, and health for spirit, soul, and body.

Breaking the Yoke

Jesus said, "The Spirit of the Lord is upon me because he has anointed me" (Luke 4:18, NIV). Jesus is the "Anointed One" of this new dispensation. That is exactly how the first Gospel preacher, the apostle Peter, understood it. He told his audience (the first Europeans to hear the Gospel) that "God anointed Jesus of Nazareth with the Holy Ghost and with power: who went about doing good, and healing all that were oppressed of the devil; for God was with him" (Acts 10:38).

The expression "the Anointed" is the same as "Christ." To say, "Jesus Christ" is to say, "Jesus the Anointed One." To the Jews the term "anointed one" meant "the Messiah." When that term was translated from Hebrew into Greek the word was *Christos,* from which we get our word "Christ." Christ is not Jesus' last name. It is a description of His office. He is "the Anointed One of God."

Now, was He anointed only while He was here on earth? If so, we should not call Him "Christ" anymore. But if He is the same, then He is the "Anointed One" today as He was yesterday. That is what He is, exactly as is said of Him in Hebrews 13:8: "Jesus Christ, the same yesterday, and today, and for ever." Not "Jesus" alone. Not even Jesus of Nazareth. But "Jesus Christ, the Anointed One."

This is also what we read in John 1:33: "Upon whom thou shalt see the Spirit descending, *and remaining* on him, the same is he which baptizeth with the Holy Ghost" (emphasis added). The Holy Spirit *remains* with Him, which is why He still baptizes in the Holy Spirit. This was an important point in Peter's first sermon in Acts 2:36. "God has made this Jesus, whom you crucified, both Lord and *Christ"* (NIV, emphasis added). Peter's preaching was after Jesus' death and ascension. Following that instance in Jerusalem which was recorded in Acts, throughout the rest of the New Testament all the way to Revelation, Jesus is called "Christ" in every major book. Ten times in the first ten verses of 1 Corinthians 1 the emphasis is on "the Lord Jesus Christ." In 1 Corinthians 2:2 Paul writes: "For I determined not to know any thing among you, save Jesus Christ, and him crucified." Just as He is still our crucified Lord, He is still our Anointed One.

If Jesus no longer delivers, no longer heals, no longer saves, no longer casts out demons, no longer baptizes into the Spirit, then we have a Jesus who is no longer "Christ," for that is the very meaning of the title and name "Jesus Christ." He is "the same, yesterday, and today, and forever." If He changed, then He forgot to tell us. But He has not changed. He is the same. Hallelujah!

7
Who Is This Jesus?

People go to church to hear about Jesus. Not politics. Not economics. Not even the man of Galilee as a distant, ideal figure. They don't want to hear about some phantom or myth. If they have read the Bible, they want to meet that same Jesus described in the Gospels. They want to meet Him again in all His glorious vitality. Preach that Jesus and the Holy Spirit reveals Him to the people not only as He was—but as He is. He will step into the midst of the crowd, just as He promised.

In my crusades, both in Africa and elsewhere, I have seen the anointed Jesus at work doing all He was anointed to do. I have seen Him sweeping into the world today with the winds of heaven. He has drawn together multitudes so great that they can only be counted by the acre. Thousands are being saved, healed, and baptized into the Holy Spirit at one time.

Why do these huge crowds come to these crusade meetings? For one reason, because I preach about Jesus—and Jesus appears and does His anointed work.

Knowing Which Christ to Preach

When I see miracles happening—miracles of healing, miracles of changed lives, miracles of cleansed sinners—I know Jesus is present. These wonders are His fingerprint, His hallmark. That was the way He ministered when He was on earth, and it is the way He ministers now through His Holy Spirit. This is the Christ of yesterday, today, and forever. Every time I use His name, Jesus Christ, it is a declaration that He is anointed to deliver. How do I know He is present in our meetings? Because miracles and wonders take place—just as they did when He showed up on the shores of the Sea of Galilee two thousand years ago. Miracles are His identity card, His genetic coding.

One misty morning, in the partial darkness, Jesus' friend John was sitting in a fishing boat pulling in his nets after a long night's work on the Sea of Galilee. Jesus was on the shore, way up on the beach, more than a hundred yards from the boat. Yet John was able to recognize Jesus instantly (John 21:7). How was he able to do this? For one reason, he recognized Jesus by what He did.

Jesus called to the men in the boat, His voice barely audible over the lapping water of the lake. He told them to cast their nets in a certain way, just as He had told them when He first met them. Once again, as had taken place three years before, their nets were suddenly filled with fish.

It must be the same Jesus, John concluded. Then he cried out, "It is the Lord!" Jesus' actions revealed His personage.

How can people know today He is the same Jesus if He doesn't do the same things He did then? How can they know Him if He is not even preached as the same One—the One who worked wonders and transformed human lives? How can anyone dare to call Him Christ and say He doesn't work miracles? His anointing guaranteed that He would be a miracle worker. Jesus is *Christ* Jesus, the anointed Jesus. There is no other Jesus than that.

Jesus can only be what you preach Him to be! The Holy Spirit can only bless what you say about Jesus. The Spirit cannot bless what you *don't* say about Him. If "this same Jesus," the very "Jesus whom Paul preacheth," is preached now, the Spirit of God will confirm it today as He did then—with signs and wonders following. Preach a limited Jesus, and He cannot be Himself. He doesn't save unless you preach Him as Savior. He doesn't heal unless you preach Him as the healer. How many are guilty of stripping our precious Lord of His anointing, just as the soldiers stripped Him of His outer garments before they crucified Him? Disbelief strips Him again of His power.

74

He is no longer mighty to save and heal in many churches today, simply because He is no longer preached that way. Using Paul's expression, He is "straightened" in our lives, which means "hemmed in with no room to work" (2 Cor. 6:12).

Making the Gospel News

An unbeliever once asked, "How can you call something 'news' which is two thousand years old? Jesus is history, not news." That unbeliever made a mistake. Only dead people are history. Jesus is alive and active throughout the world. He is a world figure, and all world figures are news, especially this One.

The word "gospel" comes from the old English, "god" (good) and "spell" (message). It is a translation of the Greek word, *evangelion.* The Gospel is not only what Jesus did, but what He does. When Luke wrote the Book of Acts he began by writing: "I wrote about all that Jesus *began* to do and to teach" (Acts 1:1, NIV, emphasis added). Jesus began to do it, and is still doing it. He is making news today.

The passing of centuries means nothing to Him. The sun is old, but active. The Bible is old, but powerful. If a telephone directory contains all the right numbers, I don't care how old it is, because every time I use a number I am getting through. I pick up the Bible, and every time I dial, I get through to the throne of God.

The Gospel is the Word of God. The great German philosopher Immanuel Kant, who possessed one of the best minds of modern times, said: "The existence of the Bible is the greatest blessing which humanity ever experienced."

But that is true only if it is preached. Yet, incredibly, there are church leaders who spend all their time studying about the Bible— studying about who wrote it, and where it was written, rather than preaching the Christ of the Bible. Meanwhile, millions die of spiritual hunger and are lost forever.

Making the Gospel Happen

If the Gospel is just left as an idea, "the letter killeth." But when it is preached under the power of the Holy Spirit, it generates power.

Under proper conditions, following the right formula, a process begins and something takes place. If you take the truth of Jesus and preach it with the power of the Spirit, you are using God's formula. Such a formula produces results. When the Holy Spirit and Gospel preaching come together, there is an explosion of power. Divine energy is released. Paul used the word *energemata*, which means "out-working energy." When such an explosion occurs, the Gospel becomes news.

When that happens, the heavenly force breaks upon us. This brings highly unorthodox and interesting effects. The graveyard atmosphere is gone! Meetings cease to be mere form and ritual. This power is not a blind force. It is Jesus at work again!

The stupefying fact about Christendom is that millions struggle on as if Christ had never been. They talk about Him as the world's most conspicuous absentee. They act as if His first advent was entirely fruitless as they struggle through life, trying to be brave and manage life's affairs. They do not realize He is here.

All around are Christ's footprints. The existence of the church is one of these, not to mention modern miracles, Bibles, Christian festivals, changed lives, restored families, and wholesome people who have been delivered from the chains of darkness. His sayings are part of our language. All that is best in civilization, morals, and principles have come from Him. Yet people drag themselves through life as if they hadn't a clue. They creep in the shadows, afraid of the dawn. They talk of wanting a new religion, but have never tried the Christian faith. The trouble is, they have built their nuclear power plants higher than their churches—depending on this world for energy while dismissing the greatest energizing force in the world—the power of Jesus.

There is growing demand for the real power, however. Too many suppose that Christianity doesn't work anymore. The church is a museum. The Bible may as well have been discovered in Tutankhamen's tomb—as if the Word were only for ancient Israel! That is why we must preach the Gospel in the power of the Spirit, with signs and wonders following. Then Jesus will step out of the Bible into modern life. Don't shut Him up in church. The church shouldn't be His tomb—although in many places it is as if the congregation is attending a wake, rather than a revival, as they sit around a casket containing Jesus' dead body. He is not dead! He is alive! He is still working His miracles today.

I have talked to people all over the world and think I have a pretty good idea what people want and need when they attend a church service. People want more than neat pulpit essays. Preachers are not called to deliver sermons, but to deliver people. *People* are the primary concern of Jesus. "I have come to set the captive free," He said. He didn't come to renovate the prison cells or to make them more comfortable with nice beds and color television. He wants people *out* of prison, not comfortable in their cells. The Gospel is not renovation, decoration, or reformation. It is liberation!

Praise God, that is how it still works! Hundreds of millions all over the world are witnesses. They testify, "The Gospel has happened to me." That is news!

How to Have the Original Power

In earlier centuries in Europe, there was a most curious trade: the selling of relics. People hawked grisly skeletons and various other items which they claimed belonged to saints. Some of them were outrageous, such as one of Noah's teeth, or the iron filings from Peter's chains in prison. But behind all this was the pathetic longing on the part of the people to touch God's reality and power. They had no idea how to do so. They tried to do it secondhand, by touching the bones and relics of apostles, martyrs, and saints. They hoped these believers' blessings would brush off on them.

But why bother? The real thing is available firsthand. Hallelujah! If we do what the apostles did, we can get what the apostles got. Peter himself said so (Acts 2:38–39). We all can know His power, and go forth garbed with Holy-Ghost might. The original brand! Pentecost is to be repeated in each life. The apostles were not extraordinary people, but ordinary people with an extraordinary God.

Plundering Hell to Populate Heaven

For more than six years I ran a Bible correspondence school in Lesotho, Africa—from 1968 to 1974. My purpose was to reach the lost people of the country for Christ. Enrollment grew to approximately fifty thousand students.

Keeping this project alive put great demands on my faith. I was only a missionary. I needed an office, and although the monthly rent was only thirty dollars, I didn't have the money to pay. I remember the day the rent came due. I prayed and groaned all day, "Dear Lord, send me the thirty dollars to pay the rent." The hours passed, evening came, and still I had no money. Slowly, I walked down the road to the house where we stayed as a family.

Suddenly, in the middle of that road, the power of the Lord came upon me. I heard His voice clearly inside my heart: *You're asking for thirty dollars. Do you want Me to give you a million dollars?*

One million dollars! My heart raced. With that amount of money I could bombard the whole world with the Gospel. Then, a different thought struck me. I am not a weepy person, but suddenly tears began running from my eyes. I cried, "No, Lord, don't give me a million dollars. I want much more than that. Give me *one million souls!* One million souls less in hell and one million more in heaven—that shall be the purpose of my life."

Then the Holy Spirit quietly whispered words I had never heard before: *You will plunder hell and populate heaven for Calvary's sake.*

That evening, standing in the dark road, a determination gripped me. By the time I reached home I knew God had greater plans for my life. The next day the thirty dollars I needed to pay the rent was given to me by a friend; but far more important, I had received a mandate from God which was to shape the rest of my life. Since then God has granted me ever-increasing blessing and grace.

How often since then have I seen the devastating power of the Gospel crash the gates of hell and blow open the dark domains of Satan! Within a single week I have seen 300,000 precious people respond to the call of salvation in our Gospel crusades. Sometimes I joke with my co-workers: "If Jesus keeps on saving souls at this rate, one day the devil is going to sit alone in hell." I'm glad to make Satan sorry.

Those who know the power of the Gospel never need to be frantic. Jesus is equal to the need. The world is sick and Jesus has the only remedy—the Gospel. Our part is simply to carry the medicine to the patients. Jesus' command, "Go ye!" is not a suggestion or a recommendation. It's an order. We have no choice but to obey. If we don't, we miss the greatest joy known to man.

How to Have an Effective Gospel

The message is Jesus. What He does shows who He is. He saves from sin. There is a legendary story of the day American President Calvin Coolidge went to church. When he got back to the White House his wife asked him what the preacher spoke about.

"Sin," the president answered in his usual clipped tone.

"What did he say about it?"

"He was against it."

People expect that. The question is—what can be done about it? People need victory over sin in their personal lives. They need to feel clean, forgiven. Many a man will tell you he knows he's not going to heaven, but he has no idea what to do about it.

We must focus on how to get people out of the mire, how to be cleansed by the precious blood of Jesus, how to receive assurance and the witness of the Holy Spirit. These are mighty themes.

I constantly stand before vast crowds. To speak anything less than the Gospel to them would be wicked. Thank God I have a Gospel, a positive message of power and hope. When the fountain of the love of God springs up, healing waters flow in all directions. This is the love that touches human hearts. Men and women open up to God. They often have little of this world's good things, but it matters less when they possess the riches of God: assurance, peace, and joy, which no factory makes, no shop sells, no affluence provides.

We are Christ's ambassadors. The Gospel is a confrontation of God with sinners. Don't reduce it to a pleasant introduction. Our message carries the highest prestige, and the most urgent priority. It is a word from the King. The Gospel preacher is not an errand boy bringing a sealed letter, but one who has spoken to the King and understands the King's mind. This is not a message for anybody who just happens to be within earshot. The Gospel is not sent only to people who have a previous religious interest. It is for all, high and low, without favor. God is saying, "I speak," and sinners should reply, "I am listening."

The Gospel is not a proposition or a suggestion. It is not thinking aloud, or an ongoing discussion. Preaching the Gospel does not mean setting forth the orthodox faith in a nice address, like an actor's soliloquy on an empty stage. It is not an alternative, but an ultimatum from the King—a mandate from God. "Believe or perish," because God "now commandeth all men every where to repent" (Acts 17:30). That is what Paul asserted. His hearers were the lofty and proud Athenian intellectuals. But Paul showed them that God, who was the unknown to them, was drawing near to them in love, stretching out His arms in welcome. The Holy Spirit takes the Word and points it as a sword straight at every individual. Doctrinal study is not the same thing. The Gospel is God's "I," speaking to our "I," as a personal communication.

Jesus the Healer

The same Lord who proclaimed liberty showed us what that liberty was by healing the sick. The Gospel is not a defense of God. God defends us. Without Him we are hapless victims of the devil. Deliverance from Satan includes divine, miraculous healing. Some have thought healing was an incidental result, a mere attachment to the Gospel. Never! It is a necessary ingredient of the message. We preach a whole Gospel for the whole man. Physical health is part of the whole package. It is God's special offer.

The Gospel is a miracle itself, and you cannot take the miraculous out of it. To preach a no-miracle Gospel results in the creation of miracle-free zones, which, regretfully, some churches are.

The Gospel is not addressed to guilty spirits, but to guilty men and women, suffering in their bodies for their sins. Jesus forgives and heals as part of the process. This is what Paul meant when he said he preached in "demonstration of the Spirit and of power" (1 Cor. 2:4). How can the Gospel be a demonstration of power if it is all spiritual and not physical? Christ is the Healer, and His healing extends in every direction—toward spirit, soul, body, mind, and circumstances.

Healing includes the authority to cast out demons. Sometimes demons may be the direct cause of sickness and depression; but not every sickness or weakness is demonic. Jesus made that distinction clear. "Cast out devils," He told His disciples, *and* "heal the sick . . . ." The anointing of God rested upon Jesus to heal the sick, and the anointing of God rests upon His servants today for the same purpose.

It is wrong to underemphasize the healing of the sick, and it is wrong to overemphasize it. One can fall from either side of a horse. Some evangelists preach only healing. Certainly, wonderful things happen wherever there is faith, but where healing is emphasized as the primary purpose of a meeting, people do not hear the message of salvation from sin. What use is it for people to be whole in body, only to be cast into hell? That is why, in our ministry, I do not advertise "healing crusades." Rather, we announce we are having a "Gospel crusade." If we put all the weight on one side of the ship, it will keel over. Yet to preach a non-healing Jesus is to present a non-biblical Jesus, just as much as if we did not preach a saving Jesus.

Jesus the Baptizer

John baptized in water. Jesus baptizes in the Holy Spirit. He is not just a "tongues" giver, or a spiritual gifts giver. He gives us the Holy Spirit. In all our crusades, we pray for people to be baptized into the Spirit. I am not ashamed of this mighty blessing. I don't keep this message in the dark "until people understand." The baptism in the Holy Spirit is part of the Gospel, and I am not ashamed of the Gospel of Christ. The apostle Peter preached the whole Gospel in his first sermon, including a strong word about the gift of the Holy Spirit. I do the same thing. The Day of Pentecost was not just evangelical. It was fully charismatic. As long as the church emphasizes the baptism in the Spirit, the Holy Spirit will stimulate evangelism and missions. As a flower carries in its blossom the seeds for new plants, so Holy-Spirit evangelism carries in itself the seeds of its own perpetuity and increase.

The Grand Finale and the New Beginning

Today's statesmen and world leaders do not know what to do, despite all the knowledge and wisdom of this latter day. Believers know. Those filled with the Holy Spirit see Jesus today, striding the continents to conquer. He will ride on in majesty, the majesty with which He was crowned at Calvary, until He is King of Kings and Lord of Lords. He is now "absent in body" but one day will return in all His glory. When that happens all the "little" kings, lords, and rulers will be pushed aside, and the world itself will be lighted with His excellent glory.

When believers come together now, they enjoy His Presence, but the world is insensitive and dead to any joy. Soon He will come, though, and all the world will know He is here again. He belongs here. He was born here. He lived here. He died here. And one day He will come again to where He belongs, to His own.

This time, unlike the first time, they will receive Him.

This puts all His work together. We cannot leave it out of our message. For a warring, stricken, frightened world, the message of Christ's second coming is the only one to spell out H–O–P–E.

Jesus is the hope of a world that has no other hope.

"Tell us," we ask the world, "how you think everything will end up? How do you think *you* will end up?"

The world has no answer, no alternative. Let the world be ashamed, not us. Unbelievers have no hope. We have—Jesus.

Preach Him! The world needs Him.

8

When the Miracle Stopped

If Jesus were to walk the land today and ask for volunteers to sign up as His apostles, there would be no shortage of applicants. "Apostle" is a noble title. But how many would want to be an apostle if they knew what they really had to do?

Apostles do not sit at the managing director's desk. The word means "one who is sent out." And what were they sent to do? First they were sent to be evangelists. Second, they were to suffer for doing it. Very few are willing to do the first. None want to do the second.

When the Lord appointed twelve men to be His first witnesses, He sent them out to introduce the Gospel to the world. Our task is to follow their lead. Today we tread where they led. Their distinction as apostles was to initiate all evangelism. Jesus gave them His teaching and they, in turn, gave it to us.

"Apostle" was not a title of honor to make them famous. It simply described what they did—that is, they went out and evangelized. This meant they were prime targets for persecution, not for prestige. In describing apostles, of which Paul was one, he wrote: "God hath set forth us the apostles last, as it were appointed to death" (1 Cor. 4:9).

These men were not divinely appointed church bosses. They left the management to others. In Acts 15 we read of a man named James who "managed" the affairs of the local church. But that James was not an apostle. James the apostle had been martyred already. The story of his death appears three chapters earlier in Acts 12. The special honor of the apostle was to be "counted worthy to suffer shame for his name" (Acts 5:41). Suffering as pioneers of Christ was the only high status they enjoyed.

In Mark's Gospel, the title of "apostle" was used because they had carried out a preaching and healing itinerary. In fact, throughout the New Testament, apostleship meant one thing only—preaching the Gospel. Paul said Christ had sent him "to preach the Gospel" (1 Cor. 1:17). He began his letter to the Romans with the clear statement of an apostle's work: "Paul, a servant of Jesus Christ, called to be an apostle, separated unto the gospel of God" (Rom. 1:1).

This was the apostles' area of authority. When Philip went out to preach in Samaria, and others were evangelizing in Antioch, the apostles back in Jerusalem first gave their approval—as custodians of the truth (Acts 8:14, 10:22). They took seriously what Jesus had told them: "I will give you the keys of the kingdom of heaven; whatever you bind on earth will be bound in heaven, and whatever you loose on earth will be loosed in heaven" (Matt. 16:19).

Infidels have assigned a strange role to Peter. They have him standing at the pearly gate entrance to heaven jingling his bunch of keys as if he were some kind of celestial receptionist. That is nonsense. The figure of speech Jesus used simply meant that Peter was to be the first to preach the Gospel on the Day of Pentecost, thereby opening the kingdom to those who believe. Peter's "keys" were the Gospel.

Indeed, the Lord made it quite clear that the keys were not exclusively in Peter's hands (Acts 1:8). The promise concerning binding and loosening was to all who believe and obey (Matt. 18:18). The loosening power of which He spoke accompanies the proclamation of the Word of God.

The apostles were honored Jesus had appointed them to carry out the task of evangelism. It was a sacred trust. They were responsible for a royal treasure. Paul later wrote of this trust in 1 Corinthians 1:17. And in Timothy 1:11, he called it, "The glorious gospel of the blessed God, which was committed to my trust. And I thank Christ Jesus our Lord, who hath enabled me, for that he counted me faithful, putting me in the ministry." Paul also declared that he was "an apostle of Jesus," who had "manifested His word through preaching, which is committed unto me according to the command-ment of God our Saviour" (Tit. 1:1, 3).

Every apostle was, first and foremost, an evangelist. But not every evangelist was an apostle. Every time the word "evangelist" is men-tioned in the Bible the two terms are distinguished. (For example, see Acts 21:8, Ephesians 4:11, and 2 Timothy 4:5.) Evangelists, how-ever, share the chief privilege of the apostle, which is preaching. Evangelists are an extension of the apostolic arm.

He Made Room for Us

The apostles thought of their task as far more than just a parti-cular job. It was the same work the Lord Himself was doing. They were not only working together with one another but "workers together with him" (2 Cor. 6:1). They were partners with Jesus—part of the heavenly crusade team of the Father, the Son, and the Spirit. The work of God Himself is world redemption, and the apostles were called to participate. So are we. God made room for ordinary men and women.

On their first mission, they jealously stopped anyone else from doing anything, but Jesus reproved them (Luke 9:49–50). Even later, they thought they had an apostolic monopoly on evangelism. But they were forced to recognize the ministries of Stephen, Philip, Paul, and the rest. These evangelists were in true apostolic succession. It is a strange apostleship which does not evangelize. It is a strange apostolic succession which does not carry out the specific apostolic task of preaching the Gospel.

Years ago I felt the Holy Spirit was urging me to visit a certain city. There were two churches in the city, so I wrote and asked for their cooperation. I received positive replies immediately. Later I heard some negative rumors, but I left this with the Lord in prayer and remained confident that I should go.

Nine months later, my wife and I arrived the day before the planned Gospel crusade. We met with the ministers to discuss arrangements with them. Our conversation just went around in circles. No matter how I attempted to guide the conversation into profitable directions, we just rambled. Discouraged and sad, my wife and I eventually went back to our hotel and had a little rest.

I must have fallen asleep as soon as my head touched the pillow, for immediately God gave me a vivid dream. It was a parable. I saw myself with the same two ministers on a sports field, of all places. We were doing the last thing that would have ever entered into my head—the long jump. One of these fellows tried first. He ran and jumped, but did not do well. The other followed and did much better.

Then it was my turn. I began the run. As I ran, I felt something wonderful. An invisible hand went underneath me and lifted me. I took off from the track and sailed gracefully—airborne. My limbs were moving as if they were running, but my feet did not touch the ground. My speed was terrific. Then I touched the jump line and ju–u–u–mped. There I was, landing at the very end of the sandpit. Marvelous! A new Olympic record! When I looked back, the other two men were far behind. In my dream, I threw my arms high with great excitement, shouting, "Oh, my God, You have made room for me!" I woke myself up shouting it.

Strangely, this dream brought me great comfort by the Holy Spirit, and I have drawn encouragement from it ever since. God makes room for us! When He sends us out in His service, He opens doors for us. We can go! We may have to take a daring leap, as in my dream, but we can take the long jump as the hand of God upholds us!. We shall land where He wants us. We'll get there!

Filling All Empty Vessels

Many churches do not see the need for the evangelist. But the true evangelist cannot work independently. One of the tasks of the evangelist, besides winning souls, is to involve other people in the same process. This can only be done if the church and the evangelist work together. Besides, the evangelist must be accountable. He needs to answer to the church for what he does. That is why I knew God wanted me to get the cooperation of the churches. Formany years my wife and I worked within the framework of a single denomination. God blessed us and used our evangelistic endeavors. However, as our Gospel crusades began to grow, God showed me another principle. I discovered it when I stumbled on the story of Elisha and the never-failing jar of oil.

> Elisha said unto her . . . Go, borrow thee vessels abroad of all thy
> neighbours, even empty vessels; borrow not a few . . . So she went
> from him, and shut the door upon her and upon her sons, who
> brought the vessels to her; and she poured out. And . . . when the
> vessels were full . . . she said unto her son, Bring me yet a vessel . . .
> And the oil stayed. (2 Kings 4:2–3, 5–6)

As I read this remarkable story I discovered the oil filled not only
the woman's own dishes, pans, jars, and bottles, but the neighbors'
jars as well. The Lord then reminded me that I should not have a
burden only for the empty vessels in my own house (i.e., my denomination), but also for the empty vessels in my neighbors' houses, also.
Then I felt Him say, *Go and collect them and fill their vessels, too.*

"Oh," I replied, "my neighbors would never let me have their
empty vessels. They would think that I wanted to steal them." Many
pastors, I knew, were threatened by other preachers, afraid they
would steal their sheep—or worse, convince their sheep to give
them some of their money.

The Lord answered, *Build up an atmosphere of trust. Then they will
lend you their vessels to fill—and you, in turn, may give them back once
they are overflowing.*

That word of wisdom changed my entire perspective when it came
to me in an early-morning meeting with the Lord. In fact, it changed
my life's direction. From that time on a burden rested upon me for
churches outside my own denomination.

I believe God wants us to recognize the leadership of whatever
body He puts us in. "God sets the lonely in families . . . but the rebel-
lious live in a sun-scorched land," David said in Psalm 68:6 (NIV).

No man should become a law unto himself, whatever his stature,
place, or work. "The eye cannot say unto the hand I have no need of
thee," Paul wrote his friends in Corinth (1 Cor. 12:21). Nor can a
hand tell the whole body it can manage on its own. Even the apostles
did not have that attitude.

Every worker needs the church like a fisherman needs the boat.
The evangelist cannot sail away in waters of his own. God has set
evangelists *in* the church. Even if an evangelist is financially independent, he should not sing a solo without the backup of the

church. He should not impatiently shrug every hand from his shoulder, no matter how intensely he burns to win the world for God.

Instructed by Heaven

I've learned much by reading the life of Paul, who in his early days was called Saul. In his history of the early church Luke tells the story of Saul's journey from Jerusalem to Damascus, where he was going to persecute new Christians. Traveling along the road, he was interrupted by a voice from the throne of God: "Suddenly there shined round about him a light from heaven: And he fell to the earth, and heard a voice saying unto him, Saul, Saul, why persecutest thou me?" (Acts 9:3–4).

Saul instantly recognized this as a divine visitation. With his deep religious interests—a "Hebrew of the Hebrews" brought up at the feet of the great rabbi Gamaliel—he must have wished a thousand times for such a direct contact with heaven. In his inquiring mind so many questions simmered. Now, the moment of truth had come. What would he learn? What revelations of the will and purpose of God were about to be his?

But he was told nothing. Nothing, that is, except, "Arise, and go into the city, and it shall be told thee what thou must do" (Acts 9:6).

In the city were those he had come to haul off to prison for their "heretical" faith in Jesus as the Christ. Now he was being sent to them because he needed them. He was even to become one of them. His first instructions would come from them, not from angels or voices from heaven. At this stage in his career he learned his first Christian truth: Believers are not a hodgepodge of random elements, but a living body called the church. This truth was so important, God had him learn it first, commanding him to "Go into the city. . . . "

Saul, humbled by his experience on the Damascus road, submitted to the ministry of others. We should learn from this man's wisdom and humility. Most don't. They have a flash of light from heaven, an illumination of soul, a revelation of truth, and off they go on a huge ego trip—independent of all counsel and oversight. They think they need not bother about those "in the city." After all, they have "heard from God." But our scriptural example, Saul, shows us we should be wiser than to go off as lone rangers; for in the city they will be "told" and helped. Saul took the right direction from the beginning of his Christian life. To him the church of his fellow believers became strength and wisdom. They helped him; he helped them. The result is history. Glorious history!

We are all dependent upon one another. If the evangelist needs the church, the church needs the evangelist, just as the hand needs the body and the body needs the hand. We complement one another as do husband and wife. If churches ignore the evangelist, they shackle him. If the evangelist ignores the church, he is throwing out a lifebelt with no lifeline attached.

Thus, having heard from the Lord and being guided by Him, I consulted my denominational leaders. I shared God's vision with them. They not only understood, they were in gracious harmony with me and gave me their blessing. I was released for evangelism beyond their borders and across all denominational frontiers. Since then I have seen the oil of the Holy Spirit fill many vessels.

When the Miracle Stopped

The widow's oil miracle eventually stopped. Why? Did God say, "That's enough for you today. I can't go on indefinitely"? He certainly did not. He was still pouring even when they could find no more vessels.

The widow said, "Quick, bring me some more bowls or jars from anywhere. There seems to be no end to this." God outdid their capacity to receive. Then the miracle ended.

There always will be oil. Zechariah saw a golden lamp which never went out. Oil for it flowed through pipes coming directly from the olive tree (Zech. 4). In the Holy Spirit, we have the source of all we need. As long as there are empty hearts, and as long as we go where God wishes and nothing restricts our movements, the oil will keep on flowing—always and forever.

Some people are baptized in the Holy Spirit and they worry, fearing the experience will be temporary, the oil ceasing. The anointing abides forever (1 John 2:27). But if we operate only with the vessels in our own little kitchen, the flow will soon cease. It is no use praying for an outpouring of Spirit week after week just for our own small church—when the whole world lies outside waiting to be filled.

Solomon wrote: "There is that [which] scattereth, and yet increaseth" (Prov. 11:24). Every church should see its walls as wide as the globe, its roof covering all people on earth. Call the worldwide revival *your* revival! The scope of the local church should be universal, but it will happen only when the assembly works alongside men and women whom God has given to the universal church. Such a church will flow with Holy-Spirit blessing. If we shut ourselves in and have nothing to do with the evangelists God has set in the church, we shall be out of the river of God.

Cologne Cathedral in West Germany has a notice for tourists which reads: "This church is not a museum." It's a sign that should appear in every church building in the world. Churches are not museums—they are mission stations.

Teaspooners

When I think about the widow's oil story, I picture the sons of the woman of Israel as they hurried down the streets asking everybody, "Do you have an extra jar, a dish, a bucket, anything we can borrow to put oil in, please?"

Back and forth they went, desperately looking for containers. Maybe some carping soul complained, "How many more things are you borrowing? What are you and your mother up to?" I wonder if anyone refused to lend them something to put oil in? If so, those who didn't lend helped to stop the flow. Perhaps it was selfishness that stopped the miracle. We can keep the miracle of revival blessing flowing to all the world, or we can limit it to our own little kitchen.

All of us have to work with others. Some may criticize, but we must not be put off. The widow's sons just smiled, knowing what their mother had in mind. They continued borrowing bowls for the oil.

God wants to anoint us, not with a smear of oil, but with rivers of oil. When Jesus made wine at Cana, he didn't fill a few glasses, but made about twelve hundred pints, enough to keep them in wine for weeks—enough to bathe in wine if they wished! There was so much the bridal couple didn't know what to do with it all. Likewise, when Jesus fed the multitudes there were twelve baskets full of leftovers. God told Malachi that if His people tithed He would open the windows of heaven and pour out more blessings than they could receive. God always gives abundantly, lavishly.

If an overcautious church won't assist because it is afraid an evangelist might run off with its vessels, there will be no abundance for the local body. Ever since I obeyed the voice of the Spirit to work with all Christians everywhere—not just in my denomination—I have seen abundance in my ministry. It was like opening the sluice gates of a dam; now we are all sharing in the flowing and endless waters of the river of God. However, once we begin to calculate and protect our own little patch, the river of God's blessing is diverted. Insular people become isolated! If we want floods of blessing, we must let the river overflow!

The Evangelist's Initiative

Sometimes one has real enemies, raised up by Satan. It is demonic opposition. Often, when I'm carrying the battle inside the gates of the enemy, I realize I am surrounded by the devil's forces. But those evil legions are surrounded themselves—by the angels of God! I know that if the anointing were to be lifted, those forces would be upon me like a pack of wolves, ready to devour me in minutes. Enemies, critics, and discouragers will come, but the anointed Christian is undefeatable.

The devil, Peter told us, is like a roaring lion. Every time I read that passage I am reminded of the roaring lion that crouched to devour Samson. Samson met this young predator on his way to Timnath (Judg. 14:5–6). The lion didn't know that Samson was the anointed judge of Israel. He just looked upon him as fresh meat for dinner. But the lion had the surprise of his life—his last surprise, as it happened.

A lion's snarl usually terrifies human beings. They turn and run, making them easy prey. But when Samson heard the snarls, he took the offensive. "The Spirit of the Lord came mightily upon him" (Judg. 14:6). When the Spirit of the Lord comes upon human beings, new things begin to happen. People begin to resist the devil, and, just as the Bible promises, he flees from them. Are you timid? If you allow the Spirit of the Lord to come upon you, you shall be bold. We are like sheep among wolves, but now the sheep are on the attack. We have power to tread upon scorpions, to walk the stormy waves, even to stand in the midst of a fiery furnace and not be burned. Experiencing the Spirit makes us more than a match for doubt and intellect. When we live in Him, we possess the ability to command demons, putting them to flight and bringing deliverance to body, soul, and spirit.

So Samson, the lion's intended victim, did not flee. Chasing fleeing victims gives lions an appetite for breakfast. But Samson had no intention of being the main course for the lion's meal. Instead, he turned on the lion, and the ferocious beast found itself facing a ferocious man. Snarling over his shoulder, the lion tried to slink off. But it was too late. Mighty hands lifted him, then smashed him against the ground. As the lion lay stunned, Samson tore his body apart with his hands. Later, his carcass became a beehive.

That's the way Christians should handle the devil and all his demons. Jesus never intended for His church to be on the defensive, slinking around and trying to keep out of the devil's sight. The gates of hell—which is the dominion of Satan's government—are to be invaded. With a mighty shout the church is to face Satan, smash him to the ground, and rip him to pieces. Offense is the best defense. Instead of waiting to ward off the devil's onslaught, we have the authority to turn the tide of battle and launch an invasion of the devil's territory!

Jesus came into the world not to defend heaven, but as a conquering man of war to "destroy the works of the devil" (1 John 3:8). Christ took the battle into the enemy's camp, invaded hell, relentlessly flushed out the foe, hunted him down, drove Satan into a corner, gave him neither quarter nor mercy, bruised that serpent's head, and left him defeated and useless. Despite what the title of a famous book said, Satan is not "alive and well on planet earth." Jesus has mortally wounded him! That is what evangelism does, in the name of Jesus. Wherever the slimy trail of the serpent is, there the people of God should track down the devil with swords whetted. Give him no rest, for we are "more than conquerors through him that loveth us"(Rom. 8:37).

The best way to defend the truth is to declare it without compromise. We have not been called to apologize for what God has said, but to proclaim His Word without shame. "The sword of the Spirit . . . is the Word of God" (Eph. 6:17). To defeat the devil, preach the Gospel, but not by shouting and noise. Use your sword.

Single-Mindedness

Somebody asked an evangelist, "Why do you always preach on 'Ye must be born again?'"

"Because," the evangelist said, "ye must be born again." No evangelist looks for a message to preach. "Woe is me if I preach not the Gospel," as Paul said. The true evangelist doesn't need to get together with other evangelists and say, "Let's discuss what we should preach." All evangelists should already have the answer to that question. They have but one basic message: "Repent and believe the Gospel!" There is no possibility of a better message.

The evangelist is a man with a driving urgency, not a man with two minds. The Gospel, and nothing else on earth, is what matters. That includes fame, money, popularity, future security— even life itself.

The Evangelist's Aim

The evangelist is a gift *to* the church (Eph. 4:11) *for* the world (Luke 24:47). True evangelists are not interested in building their own denominations. Instead, their aim is twofold.

First: Their aim is to work with the local churches, to bring people into those churches and build them into stations of evangelism. Everything they do should have this as its goal: that people should be brought into the church, where the living Word of God is preached. The greatest, and even the most successful, crusades become virtually meaningless unless they are conducted in cooperation with the local churches.

Jesus' story of the good Samaritan is a lesson for evangelists. In the familiar parable, a man fell among robbers while on his way from

93

Jerusalem to Jericho. The Samaritan found him and cared for him after religious men had passed by. After tending to the traveler's wounds, the Samaritan put him on his own donkey. Then walking instead of riding, the Samaritan took the rescued man to an inn where he was nursed back to health (Luke 10:33–35).

After we lift the fallen people who have been wounded in life, we need to enlist others to help. The Samaritan found such help at the inn, where the victim was helped to regain his strength. Evangelists find help for rescued friends in the church. There converts can be nurtured and built up in the faith. There they can become true disciples. Thank God for the "inns" along the road. Thank God for the evangelist who goes out to find the victims of the devil and bring them to these aid stations. The church/inn, caring for the convalescent new convert, will have little business without the Samaritan/evangelist. The Samaritan/evangelist will simply have to repeat the rescue work over and over without the church/inn to finish the task.

It is like fishing. The evangelist brings the nets and uses the boats of the local churches. Together they launch out, and bring in a mighty catch of fish. The evangelist leaves after handing over the catch to the local church. Then he or she shakes the net, repairs it, and heads someplace else to catch more fish—to be handed over to the next church on the shore. The evangelists gain nothing for themselves, only the joy and reward of seeing the kingdom of God built up all around.

The second aim of evangelists is to proclaim the Gospel, whether the people want to hear or not. "And this gospel of the kingdom," Jesus commanded, "shall be preached in all the world for a witness unto all nations; and then shall the end come" (Matt. 24:14). God wants the local pastor to depend on other servants. The local church has problems when the pastor tries to be more than a pastor—but also an evangelist, prophet, and apostle. That is not only impossible, it is not what God intended. God wants the pastor to be shepherd of the flock, tending to them, healing them, caring for them, bringing them to maturity so they can naturally reproduce. The evangelist occupies another office—to bring sheep into the fold. The wise pastor, even one who has a heart for lost souls, learns to work in cooperation with the evangelist, whose calling is to increase the church.

Spiritual Chemistry

The Gospel has power only if that power is released through preaching. Preaching the Gospel is like plugging into a power socket. The Gospel can't be used until it is spoken. Preaching the Gospel is also spiritual chemistry. Prayer brings power, but preaching releases it. Proclamation is part of the divine plan. People are saved no other way. This is the supernatural process instituted by God for all mankind. "It pleased God by the foolishness of preaching to save them that believe" (1 Cor. 1:21). It has pleased God that man should cast a net to draw fish from the sea, for fish normally won't jump ashore—or even into the boat.

Jesus told His disciples to "bring of the fish which ye have now caught" (John 21:10). First, catch them; second, bring them. If churches let the evangelist preach, but do nothing to bring in what has been caught, the process the Lord intended has broken down. The circuit is cut.

Christ indicated that in some villages the Word would not be received; yet it still must be proclaimed. Jesus illustrated this with the parable of the sower. Not all seeds grow equally, and some do not grow at all. Why? Because of the soils into which the seed falls. In the parable there was nothing wrong with the seed (the Word) nor with the sower (Christ Himself). The trouble lay in the soil where the seed happened to fall. In some places it produced nothing (Matt. 13:18–23). Hard, infertile soil is frustrating to the sower. But true evangelists are never discouraged; they just try somewhere else.

Some preachers have no results because they preach discipleship to the lost and the need to get saved to the already converted. When a preacher works without results, he or she needs help, not criticism. Nothing succeeds like success in the worldly sense, and the successful in the church get the praise. But we have a calling to fulfill, and success is not always the test of whether such a calling is properly done. "Preach the word; be instant in season, out of season; reprove, rebuke, exhort with all longsuffering and doctrine" (2 Tim. 4:2).

Failure is not the rule, however. The Lord sent us to the harvest field. We should not waste our valuable labors on a concrete strip or on a desert (Matt. 10:14,15). He means for us to bring in the sheaves. Wait until the rains fall and the ground softens. Whatever comes, we must *go into all the world and preach the Gospel to every creature.* Some will not hear; some will. When the Gospel is preached in all the world for a witness, then Jesus said he will come as the Lord of the Harvest! So, to work—let us hasten His coming!

Part Three
Personal Drive

9
The Swimming Lesson

Not long ago I preached in Yaounde, the capital city of the Republic of Cameroon. There a landslide for Jesus took place. A whole mountain came loose, in fact, with as many as 120,000 people in a single Gospel meeting.

This is all very exciting, of course, but how can we see the whole world effectively evangelized? The Lord must have visualized it as being possible, because He commanded us to "teach all nations" (Matt. 28:19). *Nations!* I am sure that God has big plans for reaching mankind. I go back again and again to the Word, trying to understand this thought, and asking the Lord to open my eyes.

I once came to a familiar Scripture passage, much preached on, no doubt, but the Spirit of the Lord was upon me and the truth of this passage exploded anew in my soul. Do me the favor of reading Ezekiel 47:3–7 (NIV):

> As the man went eastward with a measuring line in his hand, he measured off a thousand cubits and then led me through water that was ankle-deep. He measured off another thousand cubits and led me through water that was knee-deep. He measured off another thousand and led me through water that was up to the waist. He measured off another thousand, but now it was a river that I could not cross, because the water had risen and was deep enough to swim in—a river that no one could cross. He asked me, "Son of man, do you see this?"
>
> Then he led me back to the bank of the river. When I arrived there, I saw a great number of trees on each side of the river.

For a long time I wondered what all that meant. Now I understand the waters of that glorious river represent the life-giving flood of the Holy Spirit. For many years this world has splashed around in ankle-deep water. Now, in these latter days, the water has risen and a great river of the Holy Spirit is flowing through the world. Hundreds of millions are being baptized in that river—baptized in the Holy Spirit.

What an experience! Not only are millions of people coming to know Jesus Christ for the first time, but millions are moving from the dryness and deadness of cold religion into the swirling reality of the Holy Spirit. What excitement, to discover there is more to salvation than dry religion! To discover the thrill of the supernatural life, a life full of miracles and joy! No wonder the charismatic/Pentecostal movement all over the world is growing stronger daily. God has broken the dam put up by dead religion and has loosed the mighty river of his Holy Spirit to flood the earth.

In this vision God used an angel to lead the prophet Ezekiel to the four levels of the river. Each time the angel carefully measured out a thousand cubits—equaling fifteen hundred feet. He was leading the man of God in stages.

Ankle Deep Is God's Minimum

The first stage brought Ezekiel into water that was "ankle-deep." Any kind of contact with the power of the Holy Spirit is wonderful, but do not forget that "ankle-deep" is *God's minimum!* As a German traveling through America, I am shocked and saddened to find so many Christians stuck in this position. Like thirsty people, they have found the river, knelt to drink—but have never entered the water beyond wading depth.

A wise man once told me, when I was just beginning to drive, "Never try to follow a parked vehicle." At the time it sounded like childish advice. But as I've grown older I've found many people with their motors running and their seat belts fastened, waiting in line behind a parked leader who, for various reasons, will never pull away from the curb. That leader—and all those "following" him—are going nowhere.

Don't settle for God's minimum. Sure, you can say you are better off than those who haven't even discovered the river. But that's the wrong comparison. If you are determined to compare your life with someone else, compare it with those who have entered the river—not with those still on the bank or still wandering around in the desert.

Once I was invited to speak in a prayer meeting to people who did not believe in the baptism into the Holy Spirit. I did my best, but it was tough going. The people just sat there, wordlessly looking at me with big eyes as if I were crazy. At the end the leader stood, prayed a little prayer, and the meeting was over. I was glad to get out of the room.

"What did you think of the people?" the leader asked as we walked to his car.

"It must be very difficult to swim in three inches of water," I said sadly.

This, unfortunately, is the condition of many Christians. They sit in their beautiful boats, paddling furiously, but going nowhere—because they are grounded on the bottom. No wonder things are so hard and wearing for them.

Charles Haddon Spurgeon once wrote that "some Christians sail their boats in such low spiritual waters that the keel scrapes on gravel all the way to heaven, instead of being carried on a floodtide."

What a nightmare!

This is why so many Christian workers are frustrated. They love Jesus and work their fingers to the bone for God's glory. Yet so little happens. Why? Because they are rowing too close to the shore. They've not done as Jesus told His disciples, to "put out into deep water" (Luke 5:4, NIV). They are "do-it-yourself" people. They've left the shore and gotten into the boat, but either they've never cast off from the dock or they are resting on the bottom—rowing furiously, doing nothing but stirring up the mud.

That is not the way of Pentecost. Jesus told His followers: "I tell you the truth, anyone who has faith in me will do what I have been doing. He will do even greater things than these, because I am going to the Father" (John 14:12, NIV). He insisted we would do great works because He would send the Holy Spirit, who would do God's work through us.

101

The Lord does not hand us a toothpaste tube from which we might squeeze a little drop of power once or twice a day—just enough for our spiritual survival. The normal Christian life is one of spiritual abundance. This is what David meant when he wrote that the Spirit-filled man "shall be like a tree planted by rivers of water" (Ps. 1:3).

God wants to write a shout into your life: The success of the Christian is in the fullness of the Holy Spirit. Hallelujah! By the grace of God, I have been shown the secret of the abundant life. This is what it is: If you move into the deeper water of the Holy Spirit, that flood stream will change you immediately.

God's Personal Approach

As I was resting between preaching engagements in Africa I asked the Lord to show me why the man with the measuring rod took Ezekiel only one thousand cubits at a time, in four stages. Why not take the plunge of four thousand cubits all at once? As I prayed I felt the the Holy Spirit giving me an answer to my question. The Father is very understanding of each of His children. Unlike ignorant and cruel earthly fathers who think the way to teach their children to swim is to drop them headfirst into the deep end of the pool, God doesn't "throw us in at the deep end." He does not want to scare us to death. He is a tender, gentle, loving heavenly Father. He wants us to swim, but He has great patience. He wants us to love the water, not be terrified of it. He wants to teach us that the water will hold us up if we cooperate with it. We don't need to flail it with our arms, choking and gagging in fear. He wants us to discover we can float before we swim.

That's the reason the angel was instructed to first "measure"— then move. Our blessed Lord individually measures our capacity—then He leads. If Ezekiel had been led four thousand cubits all at one time, he would have drowned. But God very wisely instructed the angel to take him one step at a time—in four stages— into the depths of the Holy Spirit. Similarly, the Lord brings us along gently. He wants us to enter the water, but not to rush in brashly. We should have neither cold feet nor hot heads.

Learning to Swim

One day God said to me, *Do you know what it means to swim?* The voice was inner, but real—a voice I recognize so well. Well, I'm a good swimmer, so I thought I knew. But did I? Obviously God wanted me to know more. I closed my Bible and sat quietly listening to His voice:

"When you are swimming you are in another element—an element foreign to you. In the water a new law goes into operation. You cannot function as you do on dry ground. You have to let go and rest fully upon the waters of the lake. Those waters carry you."

Suddenly I saw the comparison. When I am "in Christ" I am swimming in the Holy Spirit. His waters carry me; the Spirit lifts me. Swimming takes the weight off my feet. It gives my back a holiday and lets my joints go on vacation. When I am in the dimension of the Spirit, God does the work—not me.

If you try to live the Christian life and rely upon your own strength, you severely handicap yourself. Depend on your own energy and ability, and you will be trudging wearily along the river bank, right beside the very waters which could bear you up.

So many are working for God, when God wants to work for them. I once saw a gravestone in Germany, the monument to an industrious man. Under the man's name was his epitaph, which read, "His life only consisted of work."

I said to my wife, "That is an epitaph for a mule, not a man." God didn't intend for us to be beasts of burden, or to labor like robots. He could have created pack horses to rule the world if He had wanted that. But when the Lord thought of you and me, He had something in mind other than slaves. Our Father wanted sons and daughters with whom He could enjoy fellowship. He created us to feast with Him at His table, sharing all He has with us. "All that I have is thine" (Luke 15:31), the father told his hard-working son who complained about the lavish reception over the Prodigal Son's return. God is still saying that to those of us who do not know how to sit back and enjoy His abundance and His love.

It is time to change the negative image of the Christian life. Do you sometimes feel that becoming a Christian has bowed you down?

Made your life more burdensome? Heavy? You never seem to feel good enough. You don't pray long enough, or work hard enough, or love deep enough, or read your Bible often enough? Do you feel you're never quite able to match up to God's standard? That you never seem to be able to please Him? Feeling that way, do you heap on yourself more duties—none of which bring fulfillment? You need to be borne along by the Spirit in the glorious river of God. When you swim in those waters, you are more than a conqueror.

Do you remember the story of Joseph, who was placed in an Egyptian prison for refusing to sin? Later he was taken out of that prison cell to rule. From the story of Joseph we learn we are not to *endure* but to *enjoy* the Christian life. I don't want to arrive in heaven only to discover I've been operating on only 5 percent power when I could have been operating at full throttle. As God led Ezekiel from minimum power to maximum energy, so He will lead us—if we allow Him to do so.

Life Isn't a Row of Beans

The Bible has little to say about the sea. Jonah had some problems there, and Paul was shipwrecked on his way to Rome; but the Bible is not necessarily a seagoing book. The Bible does have much to say about rivers, however. One of the great "river passages" is found in the Book of Revelation where, speaking of things to come, John wrote: "He shewed me a pure river of water of life proceeding out of the throne of God" (22:1). In Scripture, the sea stands for "the wicked" who are "like the tossing sea which cannot rest, whose waves cast up mire and mud" (Isa. 57:20, NIV). It is spoken of as the dumping ground for all our sins. Like the waters along polluted coastlines, the same old water comes back day after day, dumping on the beaches of our lives the rubbish you thought had disappeared with the outgoing tide.

But a river is different. There's a constant freshness about a river, because it never has the same water. In the same way, God has something new every morning.

When the pop artist Andy Warhol painted a picture to represent the modern age, he mocked it with an exact representation of a row of identical cans of beans. His work was biting satire. The world's diet, as he saw it, is canned (or perhaps bottled!) entertainment. There is not a single fresh item in the devil's supermarket. Yet to all who come to Him God promises "a land of rivers." He puts us under His waterfall.

A River of Power

Ezekiel was not satisfied with wading—even in knee-deep water. He could hardly wait until the water was over his head—deep enough to swim in. All who discover this secret will have their lives and ministries transformed. A few years ago, a completely frustrated minister of the Gospel came to see me. He had just come from the psychiatrist and said that he no longer could carry the load of his church of fifty members.

"The psychiatrist agrees," he said sadly. "It's just too much."

"Are you baptized in the Holy Spirit?" I asked.

"No," he replied, with a quizzical look on his face. "My denomination does not believe in it."

I took time to explain to him this wonderful truth. Then I asked if he wanted me to pray for him to be baptized in the Holy Spirit. That evening, when he left to go home in his car, he was not driving—he was *swimming*. He had plunged in and now realized God would not only give him the ability to carry the load of his fifty members—God would carry the load for him.

How big is God's maximum? No one has ever found out—for the limit always exceeds our vision. I certainly don't claim to have arrived at God's maximum. But I am definitely in transition! I am going from faith to faith, from glory to glory.

That is Holy-Ghost progression.

The Surprise That Followed

After Ezekiel swam, he returned to the river bank. This is, in New Testament terms, no anticlimax. You see, once we have been *in* the river, the river is now *in* us. Out of your innermost being "shall flow rivers of living water," as Jesus told the woman at the well (John 7:38).

The experience in the river had transformed the prophet Ezekiel, but there was more to come. When he got back to the river bank another experience was waiting. "When I arrived there, I saw a great number of trees on each side of the river" (Ezek. 47:7, NIV). Why was that so special? Why did he wipe his eyes in wonder? The trees were not there when he entered the river. They appeared only after he returned from his swim. Here's the greatest truth of this chapter: Not only did God change Ezekiel in His river, but He changed the entire landscape at the same time. In short, conditions change with anointed people and an anointed church.

We can suppose that Ezekiel had tried for many years to plant trees alongside the river, with dismal results. Despite his efforts of planting, cultivating, fertilizing, watering, and protecting, the trees always perished. Why? Because it was Ezekiel doing it, busily trying to do the Lord's work in his own strength. Then Ezekiel entered the water and discovered that all lasting, enduring work is done by God, not by man. Returning to the bank he then discovered how God does this on earth—as well as in the Spirit. In a matter of seconds God had brought forth trees—trees that Ezekiel had tried to bring forth for years in his own strength—and failed.

This is faith for today. Great things, lasting things, are never done by the sweat and energy of man—but by God's Spirit. That is what the prophet Zechariah meant when he told Zerubbabel, the builder, who was in despair over how to rebuild the temple, "Not by might, nor by power, but by my spirit, saith the Lord of hosts" (Zech. 4:6).

People who flow in and with the Holy Spirit have reason to wipe their eyes every day, because the Lord is doing wonders. And praise the Lord, nothing diminishes in God! Everything is getting more wonderful by the day.

Divine Energy

A final, important detail must be noted. Those trees which Ezekiel discovered on his return to the river bank were not only full grown, they were covered with ripe fruit. While Ezekiel was discovering the depth of the river of the Holy Spirit, God was planting and growing the trees "in no time." God is the Creator of time, therefore He controls it and is not controlled by it. He can expand it if He wishes. He can shrink it whenever He wishes. "Fruit trees of all kinds will grow on both banks of the river . . . . Every month they will bear" (Ezek. 47:12, NIV). It was as if the fruit were beckoning him, calling, "Ezekiel, come over here. No more cooking using your own recipe. God has spread the table for you. No more disasters in your kitchen! A balanced diet awaits you!"

How wonderful! Suddenly the man of God was, and is, in partnership with the Holy Spirit. No more scheming until we are steaming. No more groping in the dark. This is the wonder of a life and ministry in the Holy Spirit. This is how our world will be won for the Lord. Holy-Ghost evangelism will win our generation for God! It all begins when we are obedient to the prompting of the Holy Spirit and follow Him out into the depths, where the waters are deep enough in which to swim.

In Our Element

The Christian who is not in the river of the Holy Spirit is out of his element. We are not called to be desert dwellers, like the people of Israel were for forty years. The Lord had promised them a land of rivers, but because of little faith they remained in the desert until a new generation of fearless, faith-filled young men and women arose to take the Promised Land. Just so, Christ has promised us rivers, not as a rare exception, but as part of our natural environment. We are not to be bank sitters, admirers of the passing waters, but river walkers instead.

Many times people have told me that, under their circumstances, they could not live a victorious Christian life. One young man in Africa explained that his grandparents and his parents were all witchdoctors, and it therefore was impossible for him to live with Jesus in that place.

However, not one of us could be victorious anywhere in this sinful world, were it not for the Holy Spirit. Wherever we go, He is there. We move in Him and live in Him. He is our environment. We are baptized into Him. We are swimming in the river of God, not in a little pool He created for us that is one day likely to dry up.

Wondering if a person can live "in the Spirit" while remaining subject to earth's circumstances is like asking whether a person can live on the moon. The answer is both no and yes. Humans cannot live on the moon if they go there as they are. But, if they arrive on the moon dressed in space suits, and breathing the same air found on earth, they can live. Wearing space suits, astronauts walked, rode in a vehicle, and jumped up and down on the moon's surface.

You cannot expect to live a successful Christian life if you are not in the Spirit, for that is how God has arranged for you to live. Wherever we are, we can be in the Spirit. Bill Nelson, an American Congressman, flew in space as an astronaut aboard one of the shuttles. In his book, *Mission, An American Congressman's Adventure in Space,* he wrote that the Russian cosmonauts returned from space saying they looked and did not see God. Nelson, a Christian, said he looked and saw nothing *but* God. Even in outer space, he found himself immersed "in the Spirit."

We can be on the moon physically or metamorphically speaking, but to sustain our life we must breathe the air of heaven. Even in the worst places, foul with the breath of hell, we ourselves are enveloped in God. "He that dwelleth in the secret place of the most high shall abide under the shadow of the Almighty" (Ps. 91:1). God is our dwelling place—in every circumstance.

In our element of the Spirit we are unconquerable, invulnerable, going from victory to victory because our lives are hidden with Christ in God. God has a plan for us. His plan calls for every man, every church, every evangelist, every pastor, every worker to move in the Spirit. That is the only formula I know for success. In the Spirit of God, we can win the world for Jesus.

10
Passion Power

The law becomes love on the lips of Jesus. There are ten commandments, but the first and only commandment for Him is, "Thou shalt love the Lord thy God. . . . and the second is like unto it, . . . thy neighbour as thyself" (Matt. 22:37, 39). Horeb thundered under the weight of the Almighty when the law was given—but only with passion, for God was revealing Himself.

Who was this God, whose words at Sinai burned themselves into the very rocks? Before giving the commandments He identified Himself, establishing His right to give commandments. "I am the Lord thy God, which have brought thee out of the land of Egypt, out of the house of bondage" (Exod. 20:2).

That's who He is! The God who is a "consuming fire" is one of compassion. He had come down to deliver an ungrateful rabble of slaves from servitude. He was set only on giving them nationhood and a new country. Such a task would make great demands on His inexhaustible patience.

The Image of Love

I've often wondered if, when God made man, He shared His eager thoughts with the angels? If He had, would those spirits of wisdom have hesitated? "Such frail creatures of flesh?" the angels might have asked. "Do You think Lucifer and his evil demons could deceive them? Is it possible the devil might and lead them to destroy one another?"

The God of all knowledge knew how it would be. The first man ever born would murder his brother. But God had a master strategy which would begin with Eve and continue with all women. Woman's instinct would be preprogrammed. Within the nature of each woman would be planted a mother's heart, the purest form affection can take, an affection which never seeks reward. It would filter through to the family and set protective standards around the children and family members. Then the great secret plan of God would slowly begin to develop. It would work its way through all the ways and woes of Israel. At last it would be revealed in the Son of His bosom. "For God so loved the world, that he gave his only begotten Son. . . " (John 3:16).

The Bible says man was created in the "image of God." God's image in man was the image of love—for God is love. However, before that image could be lived out on earth, the storms of sin ruffled the waters and the reflection was distorted. But God was not outwitted. He invested all He had to see that image restored. The Gospel—the Good News—is the simple message that Christ has come to set men free from the bondage of sin and to restore, to all who accept Him, the true image of God.

For Us and to Us

Here is the meaning of evangelism: God loving us through His Gospel. Every message preached should be winged with love. We are people loving people by God's imparted love. Impassioned men and women through the ages have lived and died to preach Christ and His salvation to all tribes and nations. The finest human works have come from that same divine force: churches, charities, hospitals, orphanages, civilization itself. The love of God in a human being's soul is infinitely stronger than any other motive which has ever driven us to do good.

What was left when the presence of God departed from Mt. Sinai? The answer is found in Exodus 21:5–6—another love law. A bond servant was different from a slave. A slave had no rights. He was a slave for life and his children after him were slaves to the same master. A bond servant, however, had the right to leave his master after he had worked off his indebtedness. Yet if a bond servant married a wife who was a slave or another bond servant, he could not legally take her with him after he had served his contract with his master. He could keep his wife only if he stayed with his master in permanent servitude.

The bond servant who chose to stay with his master went through a strange but agonizing procedure. He would be taken to the front door of his master's house. Then the master would take a small spike, place it against the earlobe of the bond servant, and with a hammer literally nail his ear to the doorpost of the house. The spike would be immediately withdrawn, of course, and the man was then free to move about. The scar remained, however, as a symbol that he had chosen to stay with his master.

The scar would also be a sign—like a wedding ring (only far more dramatic)—saying: "I love my master and have given myself *for* him so I can give myself *to* him."

Nothing Other Than Love

That is the parable of the love affair God has with mankind. He gave Himself *for us* so that He could give Himself *to us*. The Savior volunteered to be nailed to the cross at Calvary. The marks of the nails in his hands and feet are the symbols of God's love for us—the symbols that He chose to purchase our freedom by His own sacrifice. "God so loved the world," Jesus said, "that He sent His only begotten Son." God is love, and that's what this world is all about. That is why we were born—to love and be loved. To know the love of all loves is the secret of all secrets. Know that, and you possess the answer to the meaning of life. A loveless Gospel is a contradiction—a sea without water, sun without light, honey without sweetness, bread without substance. The Gospel is nothing other than the message of God's love for us.

From Genesis to Revelation, the love epic moves from eternity to eternity. Over and over we hear God say: "I have loved you with an everlasting love."

Hosea, a prophet during some of the darkest years of Israel's history, heard the cry of God when the entire nation of Israel had turned its back on Him. They were wandering in the darkness of their long historical night. Hosea, however, a simple man who loved God, was permitted to catch the echo of the divine anguish. He cried out as he repeated the words of God, "How shall I give thee up, Ephraim . . . ? My repentings are kindled together" (Hos. 11:8).

Compare these utterances of a loving God—a God who loved even a people who did not love Him—with the life of Jesus. Why did Jesus heal the sick? Why did He feed the hungry multitude on the shore of the Sea of Galilee? Why did He cast out demons and set tormented victims free from their bondage? There is only one explanation given in the Bible. He had compassion. Love is all there is to the Gospel. Remove love from the universe and you have nothing but chaos. Love is the one thing that holds everything together.

Niagara of Love

Back to that question I wondered about earlier: Did God consult with the angels when He created this earth? No one knows, but from what we know about angels we know none of them ever questioned God's wisdom or purpose. No angel would have ever asked the Lord why He proposed to make man the way he is—with freedom to choose evil and the power to break God's heart. The angels *knew* why God did it that way. They knew that whatever the pain man would cause God, the Father would continue to pour Himself out in a Niagara of love.

That is the way God wants us to respond to those who turn their backs on us—with a Niagara of love.

Hell is an awful and mysterious place. It is not a subject given us to enjoy. Nor are we to use hell as a threat to those who reject God's love. Jesus never dangled men over the pit to see them squirm simply because they were enemies of righteousness. Why, then, are we even told about this possible destiny for sinners? We are told in order to arouse our deepest pity and to drive us to care about and warn the heedless.

The Love Expression on His Face

Jesus said more about hell than any other spokesman in the Bible. In fact, with a few exceptions, He is the only one who ever talked about it. Often, when I am reading His words, I wish I could have been there and heard the tone of His voice as He talked about hell.

How did He say, "Woe unto you . . . ," when He was talking to the Pharisees? What was His accent, the look in His eyes? How did He gesture? How did He express the agony He felt for His creatures? No actor could imitate it, for it sprang from a divine heart too deep to fathom. Only His love shed in our hearts could possibly give our voices the pity of His warnings.

Love Motive

If love was not the motive of the Son of God who came among us, what was? Look at these familiar words from Scripture: " . . . who for the joy that was set before him endured the cross, despising the shame . . . " (Heb. 12:2). Bible scholars, those who understand the original language, tell us that the word "for" in "for the joy," is a preposition better rendered "instead of." It does not mean "to seek joy," but *"to sacrifice joy."* After the Cross, Jesus only regained what was His already. He, the thrice-blessed God, had exchanged His crown for a cross.

That same idea is repeated again in John 13:1 when John says it was time for Jesus to "depart out of this world." *But He didn't go.* Instead, He took a towel and washed the feet of His disciples. Then he allowed Judas to go out and betray Him. He went all the way to Calvary, and became a ransom for all the devil's captives. Then, in the last half of the same verse, John explained why: "Having loved his own which were in the world, he loved them unto the end." Jesus had a mission to complete. He had to finish the perfect sacrifice. He could, having completed His teaching mission, have simply returned to the Father. But there was more. He had to go all the way to the cross, giving His life as an atonement for our sin. Only by doing this could mankind be set free. The Cross is the fulfillment of all the love promises of the Bible, for it is the Creator giving Himself in sacrifice for His creatures. There is no greater love than that.

Illustrated Compassion

The word "compassion" is one of the most unique words in the Bible, used only when talking about God and Jesus. It means "feelings toward the needy." The following is one occasion when it is used.

Jesus told a wonderful story about a father who had a son who left home in rebellion, determined to have a good time in a far country spending his father's money. Silly fellow. The world calls the story the parable of the Prodigal Son. But Jesus did not tell the story to remind us of the foolishness of sin and what it does to people (although that is surely a part of the parable). Rather He told the story to remind us of the everlasting and undying love and compassion of God.

In His story we find the father getting up each day watching beside the road—waiting for his wayward son to come home. The father in Jesus' story was *our Father.* Day after day he stood beside the road, or perhaps climbed up in the watchtower in the middle of his vineyard, his eye peering down the road toward the distant hill over which his boy might one day reappear. When that wonderful moment came, the father ran. *Ran!* It is the only time in the Bible when the image of God is pictured as being in a hurry! He was running to greet his repentant son who was on his way home.

The father in Jesus' story was an old man. He had not done any running in many years. But at that moment, when he saw his son coming "afar off," new life and strength came to those old legs. Love drove the father to get to the boy before his son had a chance to change his mind and turn away from home. In my mind's eye I can see him, racing down the road, his robe flying in the wind, his sandaled feet pounding the dust as he leaps over the rocks, his arms outstretched, and tears running down his face—taking ten steps to every one his son is taking. He is welcoming him home again, rejoicing that "My son, once lost, is now found."

What a story that is! The greatest ever told, except for the story of Jesus Himself. That once-rebellious son had been working among pigs. A Jewish boy who had fallen so low he tended swine for a gentile farmer—eating the same slop the hogs ate. Now he is returning home, wearing the same clothes he wore when he lived among the pigs. His dirty rags still carried the stench of the pigsty. But the father didn't seem to notice. He "fell on his neck and kissed him"—embracing him, filth and all. Affection overcame revulsion!

Love Restores Relationships

Is it so surprising that the elder of the two sons disowned this unwashed tramp? He said to the father with a sneer, "This thy son . . . . " The loving father gently reminded him, however, that the prodigal was more than his son—he was the elder son's brother. Love restores all relationships. That's the Gospel. The older brother accused the younger of wasting his money on prostitutes. That was his own supposition. It had not been mentioned before. It makes you wonder if that's what the elder brother would have done had he been in the same situation. But the father did not demand to know whether the allegation was true or false. He did not ask what the lad's sins were. He only saw his son's plight. Here was a lost man needing to be loved back into life.

It would take time, but the prodigal had done all he could do. He had come home. The father's response was to forgive—opening the door for restoration.

I understood this story better when I discovered that one cannot have compassion without having a physical reaction involving the internal organs of the body. We say, "my stomach turned over," or "my heart stood still." When Jesus gazed upon needy people He was *moved* with compassion. Something happened inside Him. His compassion was no mere condescending act of charity. It was the irresistible instinct in a mother or father to snatch a child back from danger. His compassion was so real it caused his body to react.

That is why He troubled Himself with universal sicknesses and the sea of human ills so long accepted as an unalterable fact of life. He reached out to those the world called "terminal." He cared for those the religious leaders said were under the "judgment of God."

True, many things resulted from His miraculous healings of the sick, including the confirmation of His own divinity. But that was not why He healed. His purpose in healing was to heal—simply that. I do not play the piano to prove that I have fingers, although that is also true. I play the piano because I love music. The purpose of music is music. The purpose of goodness is goodness. The consequences are mere side effects. Jesus never exploited human suffering for His own glory. What could He gain from His works of mercy? He did not need to come for His own profit. Why did He go to Bethesda among that litter of sick humanity who were cast up like flotsam and jetsam on a forgotten shore? Why should He go to Nain to meet a dead man—or come to earth at all, for that matter? There was no possible benefit or profit to Himself. The truth is this: He had a fatal attraction for the wretched—an attraction which led Him to a cruel death. Had He just let things alone . . . had He not healed the sick . . . had He not reached out to those in need, the world would have left Him alone. He could have taught His message and lived a long and honored life as all the other teaching rabbis of the day.

But Jesus could not do just that. He could not teach about love without applying love. He could not feel compassion without acting on that compassion. He brought His healing touch to broken lives regardless of what it cost Him. In the eyes of Jesus, the Bible says, the multitudes were as sheep without a shepherd and He "was moved with compassion toward them, and he healed their sick" (Matt. 14:14).

Then He called His disciples and sent them out to do a similar work. And His work became their work—to show compassion. Did they feel it as He felt it? Do we? The disciples came back excited and thrilled because they discovered they had power—that devils were subject to them. They felt what Jesus felt.

If we are disappointed when the afflicted remain afflicted, so is Jesus. In fact, we would not feel like that if He did not, for He made us that way. He heals to alleviate the consequences of sin, forgiving also the sin, for the same reason He saves. In no other way could He be satisfied. Deep satisfaction to the Lord is loving, caring, saving, healing. He gets nothing else out of it.

A Furnace of Love

God, the Bible tells us, is a consuming fire. He is all love, a furnace burning for His creatures. We take the Gospel to others for one reason: because we care. We are not to heal for the sake of seeing a wonder. We should not publicize it in a manner that glorifies us as the healer, nor should we advertise it as one might advertise a theater production. God is not in show business. He didn't come on earth to make a name for Himself. If He did, His audience would only repay Him with a nail.

God made a tree, and men stripped it of its gracefulness and turned it into an ugly cross to exhibit Him on for their derision. He put minerals in the earth and men mined them, turned them into nails, and used those nails to hang the Son of God on a cross to die. He created man, including Judas Iscariot. The wood that bore Him, the iron that pierced Him, the Judas that betrayed Him—He made them all Himself in the beginning, knowing full well what their uses would be. But He still made trees and He still made iron for human benefit, whatever the eventual cost to Himself.

Groundless Love

Our motives must be constantly purified until they are God's motives. Only the love of God in our hearts, put there by the Holy Spirit, can make that possible. God loves us so we will love others. Most of us have imperfect motives behind our ministry—motives which must be purified until they reflect the nature of God. In the end, our work will be tested as by fire, and what was a performance for self will be hay, wood, and stubble, instead of the gold and silver jewelry of love.

Do you desire miracle power for display? Occasionally some "demon hunter" comes along seeking exhibition opportunities. Others want to be known as people of prayer, or as men of great faith. Jesus said they have their reward—now, not in the hereafter.

Love cannot have reasons. It is the ultimate. God told Israel He loved them for no reason (Deut. 7:7–8). He did not love them because they were a great nation, for they were smaller even than the peoples to be driven out of Canaan. The Lord told them He loved them because of His love for them—which is no reason at all! The reason for love is love, which is God Himself. Love is not God, but God is love.

Jesus amazes me. He healed the man at the pool of Bethesda and went away and never even told the man who He was. What advantage did that healing bring Him? No glory, no fame; in fact, it brought Him trouble and persecution (John 5).

Another time He took a deaf man, and led him by the hand outside the village so nobody would see Him as He restored his hearing. He did the same with a blind man. He restored others and told them not to say a word. There is only one explanation: *He loved people.*

Profound Compassion

It is possible for men to have His ministry, but only to the degree that we share His compassion. When Jesus stood at the tomb of Lazarus, He wept. Why? Surely He knew what was about to happen— this great miracle of raising His friend from the dead. Why wasn't He excited over what was about to happen? Instead we read that "he groaned in spirit, and was troubled" (John 11:33). Later we read that He broke and wept. Why? At the grave of Lazarus Jesus saw men and women grieving—without hope. At Lazarus' tomb Jesus saw every funeral in the history of the world. He saw the king of terrors haunting mankind with death. His compassion for His friends—and for all of us who grieve—was so powerful He wept. It was this same compassion that sent Him, following His crucifixion and before His resurrection, into the caverns of hell to let all those who had died without hope know that He had met death—and conquered it.

That is the love the world waits to hear. That is what the church is all about—to spread abroad the love of Christ.

11

The Anointed Nonprofessional

We do not learn God's lessons with our heads. Our I.Q. has nothing to do with our spirituality. King David, for instance, discovered deep spiritual truths as a small shepherd boy, tending sheep for his father on the barren hills of Judea. We see these principles in action in his encounter with the leader of the Philistine bandits, a giant named Goliath.

David's power over Goliath, in this familiar story, lay in two equally important elements—faith and anointing. The exciting Bible story contains four principal characters (or groups of characters), all of whom illustrate the facets of spiritual warfare. I will make labels to identify them.

- David: the anointed nonprofessional
- Israel's worrying warriors: the unanointed professionals
- King Saul: the ex-anointed professional
- Goliath and the Philistines: the anti-anointed professionals

The Anointed Nonprofessional

David was not a professional warrior, but he was an anointed man. He did not belong to the IDF—the Israeli Defense Force. He did not have rank or training as a soldier. He was a humble shepherd boy, who, much like the Bedouin shepherds in the Sinai today, spent all his time walking around the hills with his small flock of sheep and goats. He used his little slingshot to fight off the wild animals. When the sheep were resting he would play tunes on little pipes made from reeds, or perhaps he would sing songs as he strummed his harp. His job was minding sheep.

Then came the day when his father asked him to carry food to his brothers serving in the Israelite army, the day he gate-crashed history—an act of breathtaking audacity. But his anointing from God was his credential to do what he did.

The anointed David was at this point nothing more than an appointed errand boy. The Lord's anointed should always be willing to be errand boy. If we are faithful in that which is least, the Lord will make us rulers over much. The anointing of God can rest on the humblest of workers.

David had never seen a battle, nor a battlefield, before he arrived in the valley of Elah. He came, however, with anointed vision and boundless faith in the Lord. When he arrived at the front, however, he found the soldiers—from the generals to the buck privates— nothing more than worrying warriors. There was no spirit of faith or victory—only grief, despair, and calamity.

The moment he opened his mouth to ask a question, he bumped into his eldest brother, Eliab. David was merely a teen-ager and Eliab was a professional soldier, a captain in the army. Eliab, you remember, was the first of the sons that old Jesse, David's father, had brought forth when the prophet Samuel came to their house saying God had told him that numbered among the sons of Jesse was the one destined to be the king of Israel. But Samuel had not anointed Eliab. Nor had he anointed any of the other older boys. He waited until little David came in from the field. It was then the Lord said, "Rise and anoint him; he is the one" (1 Sam. 16:12, NIV).

Eliab was an unanointed professional who represented the whole army of unanointed professionals. Who knows how many today believe they are in God's army—but lack the anointing?

There was bound to be friction between the anointed and the unanointed. David was like sandpaper to Eliab, irritating him. Maybe it will help you understand if I point out some of the differences between these two classes, the Eliabs and the Davids.

Where the Anointed and the Unanointed Differ

Both David and his eldest brother saw Goliath and heard the blasphemies that came out of his mouth. Eliab listened with a sinking heart. But when David heard the roaring of the giant, the anointing of the Lord began to heat up within him. Goliath's words had a chilling effect on Israel's unanointed professionals—leaving them ice-cold in fear. But David began to burn in faith—and anger—at the same moment.

The anointing of God gives great boldness; it makes people fearless in the face of overwhelming circumstances. The anointing makes the difference between an academic faith and a burning faith. Let me warn you—the one faith always will irritate the other. Don't be surprised when it happens to you.

Eliab had reason on his side. But it left him weighing the balance between the Israelites and Philistines. Looking merely at the circumstances, he saw no other resources. Eliab was able to make professional assessments of battle situations, and he saw that Israel had no chance of winning.

David, in contrast, knew he had the God of Israel on his side. He felt holy stirrings and indignation within his soul. The difference was the anointing which gave him resources unknown to others. His inner eyes of faith were upon Jehovah. God's anointing upon him made him hungry for victory, excited by his eager anticipations. He did more than just hope and pray. His anointing was the earnest conviction of things to come.

Eliab was no dummy. He had made an excellent impression on Samuel, the prophet. At first glance Samuel was sure this was the man God wanted as the next king of Israel. But the Lord had said, "Look not on his countenance or on the height of his stature; because I have refused him" (1 Sam. 16:7). Why? We shall see.

In human contrast, David was not worth consideration. He was the youngest, a bouncy, red-headed, freckle-faced teen-ager. If he were in our church we wouldn't even let him hand out hymn books to the congregation. But the Lord said to Samuel, "Arise, anoint him: for this is he" (1 Sam. 16:12).

An unknown lad from the tribe of Judah who didn't even look Jewish. Being reddish suited the future king, however. Remember, the jewel stone for Judah in the high priest's breastplate was red.

God's favor upon David did not give him favor with his seven unanointed brothers. Now, in the battle zone, Eliab spoke for all when he angrily asked David with whom he had left "those few sheep in the wilderness."

David had not neglected his sheep. He had left them in the hands of a keeper. God's anointing does not allow anyone to neglect their proper duties. David was a man after God's own heart who did *all* God's will, even in the ordinary business of everyday duties. Not only that, he was obeying the command of his father who had sent him to the front to bring provisions for his brothers.

David, the anointed nonprofessional, could not be bothered with Eliab's miserable quibbles. They were, to him, irrelevant nonsense.

The anointing of the Holy Spirit within him now reached the boiling point. He ignored mere protocol. If there was nobody to face Goliath, then he, a nobody, would face him. He would do it in the name of the Lord, because he knew the God of Israel was incapable of inaction! The army considered David an outsider, but he, David, knew he was God's insider.

Face to Face with the Ex-anointed

Maybe, David wondered, *I opened my mouth too wide by questioning the army's policy. After all, it's none of my business.* Yet he knew, deep inside, it *was* his business. Somebody had to face the champion from Gath. If the soldiers wouldn't, then he would. And because of that, he wound up in the tent of King Saul—saying, "Let me do it if they won't." It really wasn't faith speaking as much as it was the anointing.

David recognized Goliath as his own enemy, not just as the army's target for the day. Here was the deadly foe of every man, woman, and child in the land. Getting rid of him was everybody's business, army or no army. The same applies to the devil today. It's every Christian's business to put him out of business. The kingdom of God can't be run only by professionals paid from church funds. Anointed nonprofessionals are needed, because the devil is a menace to everyone.

A battle needs supplies and money, some of which David had come to bring. Dollars, though, are no substitute for dedication. David could not stand around any longer as the soldiers seemed content to do. He was different. He was anointed! The moment he showed any interest in taking on the giant, eager hands pushed him forward. No doubt Goliath would make mincemeat of him, but it would break the deadlock. A nobody like David didn't matter anyway. He could be offered as the sacrificial lamb. Then Israel could get on with the main battle.

To Saul and his generals, who had been staring at the deadlock for days, it seemed to be a joke. Here was a raw lad from the country proposing himself as the defender of Israel. But the fact was, when Samuel the prophet had anointed the shepherd boy David, King Saul had become the ex-anointed of the Lord. Now the anointed and the ex-anointed stood face to face. When Saul looked at David with amusement, he saw that the boy was quivering. But David's quivering was not from fear, it was from a powerful Holy-Spirit anointing.

"You can't fight Goliath!" the ex-anointed king sneered. "Do you know what you are up against? Have you seen how big he is? You don't know the first thing about combat. Goliath has been a warrior all his life."

There are always those who try to push others out, and those who push others in to do what they are afraid to do themselves. Eliab wanted to freeze David out, but you can't freeze fire. If the army had voted, David would not have received a single ballot. But David's success did not depend on his popularity, nor the approval or confidence of others. It depended on one thing: the anointing of God.

The Ex-anointed

Satan was once anointed warrior, but he became the ex-anointed when he rebelled against his Commander-in-Chief. Since then he has been the captain of all the ex-anointed. That remarkable story is told in Ezekiel 28:14:

> Thou art the anointed cherub that covereth; and I have set thee so: thou wast upon the holy mountain of God; thou hast walked up and down in the midst of the stones of fire.

Thou wast perfect in thy ways from the day that thou wast created,
till iniquity was found in thee. . . . Thine heart was lifted up because of
thy beauty, thou hast corrupted thy wisdom by reason of thy bright-
ness: I will cast thee to the ground. . . .

Isaiah the prophet gives additional light when he writes:

How art thou fallen from heaven, O Lucifer, son of the morning. . . .
For thou hast said in thine heart, I will ascend into heaven,
I will exalt my throne above the stars of God. . . . I will be like the most
High. (13:12–13)

In a sense the devil had faith. "The devils also believe, and
tremble" (James 2:19). But just knowing about God and believing
about Him is not enough. The one thing Satan lacked was the
anointing. It had departed, leaving behind only the evil husk of a
once-illustrious being.

King Saul was a pathetic reflection of the same condition. Just as
Satan pursued Jesus to kill Him, Saul soon pursued the anointed
David. In both cases, a kingdom was at stake. The ex-anointed always
will persecute the anointed of the Lord. Satan is not like Jesus, who
"thought it not robbery to be equal with God" (Phil. 2:6). Jesus was
"obedient unto death, even the death of the cross . . . Wherefore
God also hath highly exalted him, and given him a Name which is
above every name" (Phil. 2:8–9).

David was undaunted by King Saul. Although he had never fought
as a professional soldier, he had fought wild beasts, the predators
that were always after his flock. A bear and a lion had come—
and ended up wishing they hadn't. Goliath was a one-man war
machine, a human tank; but in David's view he was too big a target to
miss. With God on his side, David felt like a whole armored division.
Writing of his confidence in God, he said, "For by thee have I run
through a troop; and by my God have I leaped over a wall"! (Ps. 18:29).

With David it was God or nothing. Goliath was not challenging
David, he was challenging God's honor. Goliath had thrown down
the gauntlet not merely to the Israeli army; he "had defied the
armies of the living God" (1 Sam. 17:36). That was Goliath's mistake—a mistake that cost him his head.

Saul's Armor

Saul should have been the one to fight Goliath. He was head and shoulders above the biggest men in Israel. Furthermore, he was the king, the one who had known the Lord's anointing. Then there was mighty Abner, a ferocious warrior. Yet instead of either of these two military leaders doing what they should have done, the two of them let David do it. In fact, the first thing Saul did, like unanointed professionals often do, was to make sly fun of this peasant lad who believed God could give him victory over the greatest warrior in the Philistine army. It was his way of taunting him into fighting the giant.

So King Saul smiled, winked at his brave general staff, and offered David the use of his own royal armor. What a figure David would cut, half Saul's size, parading in front of two armies in that oversized suit of armor.

The leather coat was covered with layers of leather and bronze, burying David inside. The chain mail which went over the top of it weighed him down. Imagine David trying on the bronze helmet: He could turn his head sideways and the helmet stayed forward! The size-44 belt was long enough to wrap twice around David's slim waist. Saul's sword was so long it trailed on the ground and threatened to trip little David. Goliath would die, all right—of laughter!

When the Anointing Boils

What must Goliath's reaction have been?

"Give me a man," he roared (1 Sam. 17:10). He had waited for Israel's answer. It surely would be their greatest man of war. Then, when the hero finally emerged from the ranks of Israel's mighty warriors, Goliath could hardly believe his eyes. As a roar went up on both sides, a young stripling in sandals and a farmer's smock ran across the field! His weapons were a couple of staves and a little sling. Goliath was insulted. Did Israel think they were only chasing off a dog, sending a lad with sticks and a sling?

Goliath didn't know it, but he was up against the very Spirit of God. Invisible within the shepherd lad's heart, the anointing began to boil. There was no holding back any longer. First Samuel 17:48

says David "ran" toward the Philistine champion, like an arrow released from the bow of the almighty God.

Goliath bellowed a hoarse warning at David. In contrast came the voice of the sweet singer of Israel, "I come to you in the name of the Lord."

This was not a new phrase coined by David. The Israelites used it often. But not this time. This time they were afraid. They had the Ark of the Covenant. They knew they were God's chosen people. They sang about "the Lord mighty in battle," stamping it out in rhythm until the ground shook. But on that day nobody was willing to fight Goliath. The soldiers had faith, but they did not act on it. The anointed David, however, felt the Spirit shaking him and he ran eagerly to meet the enemy—knowing God had already given him the victory.

So often God's army does everything but fight—*everything except evangelize*. Israel spent time organizing, but that was all. They polished their weapons, argued about who should be the leaders, discussed military tactics. But they did not go out to battle.

The army of the Lord is often like that, concerned with polishing up the wherefores and therefores of their constitution, discussing church order, claiming to be "a people of power," facing Goliath but never going out to fight him. One pastor told me he did not have time to evangelize, he was too busy standing before a huge map in his church office sticking pins in locations where his survey showed all the lost people lived. Every day he changed his pins around, but he never went out on the streets to talk to those whom the pins represented.

God's Bullet

David did what any soldier should have done. He fought the enemy. He turned his passive beliefs into active faith; because he believed, he tackled the giant. He did not use professional weapons, but only what he was familiar with: a slingshot. He could hit a rabbit at fifty paces, but facing a giant was another situation.

David did not make the mistake so many make today. He did not confuse presumption with faith. He knew that in order to do God's work, he needed God's anointing. It is no coincidence that the only believer in the army to tackle the enemy was the one who carried this anointing.

God is waiting for men and women of faith and anointing who will match their actions to what they believe, whose faith will make them attempt the impossible, doing what they would never do unless they believed God.

We can all do the ordinary things and trust God, just as David did the extraordinary thing and trusted God. That is what faith does when it comes with the anointing of the Spirit. When both are present, you believe the impossible—and do it.

I'm not much good with a slingshot—especially the kind you twirl around your head before releasing the stone. I have no idea how hard a stone from a sling can hit. But I do know that when it is slung by an anointed slinger, it can travel like a bullet. When David's stone sank into Goliath's forehead, prostrating him to the ground with a mighty crash, the youthful victor administered the *coup de grace* with Goliath's own sword.

Know this—your word, if it is His word, carries far more weight than all argument. It catches people where they are not protected. I rely upon that Word when preaching to thousands of people, all of whom are different. God knows best which words will reach them.

The professional enemy had prepared for every danger, but not for a stone from a sling. Likewise, God has many a surprise to spring on the devil. The enemy does not understand who, or what means, God is likely to choose. When we move in the Holy Spirit, we always strike the Achilles heel of the devil and thus defeat him. The anointed nonprofessional David stuck to his brand of active faith and gloriously succeeded.

As an anointed P.S. to the story, we note what David's faith did for others. Suddenly all the unanointed professionals of Israel, seeing how God could use a simple shepherd boy to accomplish His purpose, took heart. They charged into battle, chasing the fleeing Philistines and winning a mighty victory. Faith is infectious. It breeds more faith. But the anointing comes only from God Himself.

The Anointed Professional

God does not necessarily bless ignorance. David was ignorant of the ways of the world, ignorant of military strategy. But this was not the reason God blessed and anointed him. He anointed him because his heart was right. God can also anoint those who are educated— the professionals. When that happens even greater miracles take place. David soon became a "professional," but he was an anointed professional. Anyone who does something long enough will qualify at some time! But David never relied upon higher learning, experience, or old routines and rites. He kept a spiritual freshness through the Holy Spirit.

> There will I make the horn of David to bud: I have ordained a lamp for mine anointed.
> His enemies will I clothe with shame: but upon himself shall his crown flourish. (Ps. 132:17–18)

The "lamp" was the Spirit of Revelation, the Holy Spirit. David received new spiritual insight all the time. He relied upon the anointing of the Holy Spirit, and thus upon His Lord and God. God does not work miracles in order to save us from trouble, but to glorify His name.

Believe!

Act!

But at all times make sure of your anointing and say to the Lord, "Now bid me run, and I will strive with things impossible."
God moves with those who move.

12
Power Tools

Today, all over the world, nations are being shaken by the power of God. Old political structures are crumbling in Europe and elsewhere. Kingdoms once thought indestructible have fallen, and new kingdoms are rising. This is not man's doing, but the work of God.

The same is happening in the spiritual realm. Every place I go the crowds grow larger as hundreds of thousands turn out to hear and receive the Gospel. Lives are being revolutionized. Old structures of sin and demon possession are falling. Men and women, once under huge bondage, are emerging free. Hundreds of thousands are being healed. People ask, "What is the secret of your success?" They do not understand this is not the work of man, it is the work of God. There is no secret.

Entertainment, politics, and other attractions may draw crowds, but nothing is like the Gospel. It offers no cheap popularity, yet its wonderful power is bringing millions together in marvelous fellowship around the globe.

How does it happen? The answer is that the kind of evangelism that wins the world is Holy-Ghost evangelism. This is the kind of evangelism which makes use of the weapons God has given for this task, namely the gifts of the Spirit.

Anointed preaching, along with anointed music and singing, are not the only explanations for our success. We must have those, but the first disciples had even more. The New Testament talks about "manifestations," which were things to see. They are truths made visible.

What are the works of God? They are not only conversions, or even healings. They include revelation, prophecy, supernatural knowledge, wisdom, discernment, dreams, visions, and authority over the powers of Satan. These are the aspects of our crusades and meetings which I feel have helped attract the hundreds of thousands. People wake up to the reality of spiritual things when they see something that is beyond mere words. The gifts of the Spirit supply this slice of experience.

In this chapter I want to stress the glorious possibilities of these weapons of spiritual warfare–the gifts of the Spirit. By these God-given means, the timid soul can become bold and the defensive person can become aggressive. The Lord intends us to carry the credentials of an ambassador. To those whom He sends, He also gives this startling power and authority.

Many people yearn for these spiritual gifts but are nervous about using them. *Suppose I am wrong?* they worry. But the worst mistake is not to employ the weapons of the Lord.

Here are some key scriptures to encourage you:

Be thou strong and very courageous. (Josh. 1:7)

In the fear of the Lord is strong confidence. (Prov. 14:26)

Be strong in the grace that is in Christ Jesus. (2 Tim. 2:1)

There is one Old Testament scripture that has long fascinated me. Put alongside the New Testament truth, it gives a clear picture of how God does turn the tides and the tables on His enemies:

And Joash the king of Israel came down unto him [Elisha], and wept over his face, and said, O my father, my father, the chariot of Israel, and the horsemen thereof.
And Elisha said unto him, Take bow and arrows. And he took unto him bow and arrows.
And he said unto the king of Israel, Put thine hand upon the bow. And he put his hand upon it: and Elisha put his hands upon the king's hands.

130

And he said: Open the window eastward. And he opened it. Then Elisha said, Shoot. And he shot. And he said, The arrow of the Lord's deliverance, and the arrow of deliverance from Syria: for thou shalt smite the Syrians in Aphek, till thou have consumed them. (2 Kings 13:14–17)

Cotton-Wool Comfort

Joash, the king of Israel, was young and inexperienced when disaster threatened his kingdom. The Syrian army had mobilized against him, and he knew he had nothing to match it. He had visions of defeat and his own imprisonment. Even the possibility of death haunted him. He was sick with worry.

Joash was one of Israel's bad kings, but in his anxiety he remembered the Lord's prophet, Elisha, who was then about eighty and likely to die soon. The king, in his anguish and despair, visited Elisha. He approached him with flatteries. He described Elisha's usefulness to Israel like "the chariot of Israel, and the horsemen thereof" (2 Kings 13:14). Then he "wept over his face," letting the old prophet see his tears, crying "O my father, my father. . . ." It was quite a show!

The fact was, however, that Joash wasn't weeping because Elisha was dying, but because he might die himself. He needed help and was willing to do anything to get it.

Elisha was not taken in by all this emotion. But he did have a word from the Lord; then he simply told the king to take his bow and arrows. I think he could just as well have said, "Take your handkerchief." Elisha had seen too much of Joash's ways to be moved by his sob story. God was not impressed either. It is high time for somebody to say that God knows when people are weeping only because they feel sorry for themselves.

There are some who seem to need much more of other people's time. Often this is because it is so difficult to know what their trouble is, if indeed they know it themselves. They may occasionally be victims of mental bruising earlier in life.

Leaders who specialize in counseling may find such patients give them plenty of practice. But there is the danger that the hours devoted to them could drive the trouble deeper into the patients' consciousness, even making such folk feel they are "very special sufferers," beyond the normal ability of the Lord to help them. Never forget that *nothing* is too hard for God.

Our job is not to "cotton wool" people who already feel too sorry for themselves. Our task is to wake them up, not give them soothing pills. There is a time when people need to come out of themselves, and to see again the needs of a dying world. It is a sin to give valuable time to chronic complainers—time which seldom resolves their personality problems—and miss the time which should be given to winning the lost.

Elisha knew this. He had no time to hunt for tissues for the king's tears when national calamity loomed. He resorted to no probing inquiries, because the need was plain. He saw the king's tears were not for a dying prophet, nor even for a nation in danger, but for the king's own personal future. By the word of the Lord, therefore, without formalities for the royal presence, Elisha came straight to the point.

He said, "Take bow and arrows." He was brusque, perhaps, but when enemies are invading, there is no time to beat around the bush. It is a time for bows and arrows. A military attitude was needed. Joash had to forget himself and be a real king to his people.

Trembling or Triumphant Saint?

Where are our weapons?

Paul told Timothy to "stir up the gift which is in thee" (2 Tim. 1:6). The word Paul used for "stir up" has to do with fire. It means "to bring up to full flame." Don't cool off! Use the fan on the dying embers.

Joash was a feeble king with little fire in his bones. He went crying to Elisha, "My father, my father," when he was scared, instead of mustering his army and bringing weapons out of the armory. Elisha would have appreciated action a lot more than words covered with syrup.

We have our weapons, and the devil has done his best to stop Christians from using them. When the Pentecostals opened God's armory at the beginning of this century, the entire church rose up in alarm. Until then, preachers too often had relied on human means, and not on the power of the Holy Spirit. The use of the power gifts presented a huge threat to these powerless preachers. What would happen if the uneducated and unsophisticated preachers got more results than those with a long string of degrees behind their name? Horrors!

Many churchmen and medical doctors have opposed divine healing. They have made much of those who are "disappointed" and who are not immediately healed. They forget that doctors "disappoint" millions. Nearly everyone in the graveyard has been to a doctor first, yet nobody would be so foolish as to demand the closing of all hospitals! Church folk who object to divine healing simply because some are not healed do not minister to the sick at all. This leaves everybody unhealed! Then where is compassion, or obedience to the Scriptures?

Other gifts also have come under attack. When the "word of knowledge" was first being manifested by Pentecostal and charismatic evangelists, many declared it to be "spiritualism"—the works of the devil. Why shouldn't God do such mighty things? In fact, spiritualism and clairvoyance are the horrible counterfeit of what God means to do. The gifts of the Holy Spirit are far greater than anything the occult can produce. There must be the real wherever there is the false.

Some Spirit-filled people have let their bow and arrows gather dust in a corner because of such critics. Others have been hurt, perhaps by remarks from a fellow believer, and thus have dropped their gifts of prophecy, or of tongues and interpretation. They have "lost" them, though God never takes them back, "For the gifts and calling of God are without repentance" (Rom. 11:29). These gifts *must* be recovered. Go back to the day and the place you left those spiritual gifts, and ask the Lord to forgive you. Dry your tears of despair and "take bow and arrows" *again!*

Waiting for God's Moment

When I enter a meeting, I have my bow and arrows with me. The bow is already strung, for I am praying in my heart, *Lord, which is your appointed target? Where is the Word of Knowledge? In which direction is the*

133

anointing of the Holy Spirit flowing? Where is the key miracle for today?
That is what I mean—my bow is under tension, at the ready.

It would be tragic for a bowman to charge into battle and then
have to stop and string his bow after the fighting begins. He sharp-
ens his arrows, strings his bow, and slots his first arrow ahead of time
so he is ready at a moment's notice to fire his arrow toward the
target.

King Joash was a pathetic character. Although trained as a warrior,
his fear prevented him from taking up the weapons that he was
skilled to use. Because of his unmanly weeping he couldn't see
properly. He was so scared by the enemy threat that his hands shook.
Then something happened that changed everything when "Elisha
put his hands upon the king's hands." Don't worry, God will do that
for you as well—not because He approves of your actions, but
because He loves you and loves those you are responsible for. Ezra,
you remember, was the one who kept repeating, "I was strengthened
as the hand of the Lord my God was upon me" (Ezra 7:28). Ezra
wasn't the only one strengthened. The Bible is full of testimonies of
those "strong in the Lord and the power of His might." Glory to
God!

Having the gifts of God's bow and arrows is one thing. Using them
is another. "Prophets" should not just open their mouths because
they are prophets. They must wait for God's moment of command,
that touch of God upon their hands.

My African friends told me the story of the elephant who found
the nest of an ostrich. The mother ostrich had gone off to a river
somewhere to drink. The elephant saw her eggs uncovered, and big
elephant tears rolled down her trunk. "How can a mother be so
irresponsible and leave her eggs unprotected? Well, until she
returns, I will help out." So the elephant, with maternal concern, sat
on the nest. The devastating result was scrambled eggs. The beast
had a heart of compassion, but not a drop of wisdom in her
elephant-sized brain.

Some Christians I know are just like that.

Joash had his weapons, but it was Elisha's touch which imparted
strength. Then the king dried his eyes, and fear left him. Divine
confidence came—the same confidence that can be ours. It has

been mine many, many times. Suddenly I will know that the enemy will be beaten and his works destroyed. I am sure miraculous things will take place when I know the anointing is there, breaking the yoke. We can be strong in strength which God supplies through His eternal Son.

Open the Window

Elisha next told Joash, "Open the window eastward." Now he had his weapon and the anointed hand of the prophet on his. But you can't shoot arrows through a closed window. You need to begin to prepare and make opportunity, set things up, and clear the decks for action. By that I mean listen to the Holy Spirit in this matter, as Joash listened to Elisha. It may mean pushing aside normal arrangements, ignoring "official channels" and even courtesies, but if God says it, do it—always remembering the elephant and the ostrich! When Jesus tells you to do something, don't let anyone stop you.

I was about fifteen years of age when God first put His hands on mine and used me in a special way. I was in my pastor/father's church prayer meeting in northern Germany. We were all kneeling when the power of God came over me and I felt as if my hands were filled with electricity. I clearly heard the Lord tell me in my heart, *Arise and lay your hands upon Sister C.* I nearly fainted thinking of the consequences, for my father was a very strict man. How could I just get up and put my hands on that lady? But when I hesitated, the Lord seemed to turn up the voltage, and I felt as if I were dying. Slowly I lifted my head and peered around for Sister C. I stayed as low to the floor as I could, creeping to her so I would not be detected. Then I put my hands on her head. I was just being obedient. At that moment I felt the power of God go through my hands into her.

Father had seen me, however, and his face showed he was not pleased. He went straight to her.

"What did Reinhard do to you?"

"Oh! When Reinhard laid his hands on me, it felt like electricity flowing through my body. I am healed!"

Even my father could not argue with that.

By going to her as God commanded, I learned this lesson: Nothing else will happen until you obey the first command. Until Joash opened the window the next command could not be given.

Shoot!

Interestingly, Elisha did not say, "Take aim!" There was nothing to aim at. God just wanted him to shoot. The arrows of God are self-targeting, and will never miss. They are like pre-programmed cruise missiles. They will strike targets invisible to the human eye and no heart can avoid them.

When God gives a word of knowledge, I need not figure out whether it fits, or whether it is likely to be correct. God knows better than we know. My duty is to release the arrow from the bow, and it will become an "arrow of deliverance." The Spirit of God alone can plumb the depths of a man's own spirit. He will not slip up. The Spirit is familiar with everybody's history and with their most secret thoughts. It is not easy for the rational person just to shoot through an open window of opportunity without seeing the actual target. When he does, though, the results are amazing.

One of the overwhelming experiences I had of this kind involved my brother Jürgen. We had grown up together as sons of godly parents, but he didn't want to follow Jesus. When we became adults, he had his career and life mapped out.

Time passed. I did not know that his wife had left him, that his closest friend had died of cancer, or that his life had become meaningless to him. Then one night he dreamed. He seemed to be walking on a high bridge when he slipped and felt himself falling, crying out. Then he awoke, drenched in perspiration.

Later he said, "For the first time in my life, I had a burning desire to pray to God, remembering the scripture I had learned as a child, 'Call upon me in the day of trouble: I will deliver thee' [Psalm 50:15]. I went down on my knees and said, 'Lord, You know I do not even know whether You exist or not, but my brother Reinhard is Your servant. Give me a sign through him that You are alive.'"

That night I was six thousand miles away in Africa. I didn't know about his troubles, nor that he was considering ending his own life.

There had been very little communication between us. However, in the small hours of the morning, I, too, had a terrible dream. I also saw a high bridge and my brother walking on it in some kind of fog. The bridge had no guard rails, and I feared that Jürgen might lose his orientation and fall off. He walked on, into that fog. I dreamed that I called out in desperation, "JÜRGEN!" The next sound I heard was a voice crying out from the bottomless depths. It was my brother's voice.

I then woke up, wet with perspiration. "Lord, what is this?" I asked.

"Jürgen is on the bridge to eternity. If you do not warn the godless, I will require his blood from your hands."

The fear of God came upon me. It took some time before I wrote him an urgent letter. I had fierce battles in my own heart before doing so, but I told him of my dream. I then pleaded with him to receive Jesus Christ as his personal Savior.

On the day before Christmas 1987, I received his reply. Jesus had wonderfully saved his soul. Hallelujah! He knew his sins were forgiven. He wrote, "I am walking with the Lord every day. He has solved all my problems." When I got that letter, I could not control my emotions. I just sat there, looking at the paper, weeping for gladness.

How wonderful the Holy Spirit is! How effective are His gifts! They are God's powerful weapons. We play into the devil's hands when we are shy about them or apologetic about their use. What if I had not written that letter? What if I had never opened the window eastward, shooting that arrow into the dark? It did seem irrational at the time—acting on a dream. But the arrow found its mark because it was directed by the Holy Spirit.

In the name of Jesus, I say to you, Open your window! Push aside your fears! Let your obedience in faith overrule all your nervousness. Let go and let God have His wonderful way through you!

Joy!

When Joash shot that arrow through the casement, something happened to Elisha. He shouted, "The arrow of the Lord's deliverance from . . . Syria: for thou shalt smite the Syrians in Aphek till thou have consumed them" (2 Kings 13:17).

Joash believed it, and went forth in the strength of that confidence. Three times he overcame the Syrians, recovering his lost cities of Israel (see 2 Kings 13:25).

One mighty meeting with God changed the course of that king. That is all it takes, one meeting with God. The men and women whom God uses have had such a meeting. They have moved out of religious routine into the winds of the Holy Spirit. Any one of us can have that meeting, but like Joash we have to be desperate enough to break through. The essential ingredient is the anointing of God. Until you have that, everything is presumption. Once you have His orders, however, it is presumption *not* to obey.

Boiling Point

The story of Joash and Elisha is remarkable. But there is more. Joash could have done even better. In 2 Kings 13:18 we read that the prophet Elisha told him to take his arrows now and "Smite upon the ground." He did, three times, only it was a half-hearted effort. Elisha was "wroth with him," and said, "thou shouldest have smitten five or six times; then hadst thou smitten Syria till thou hadst consumed it: whereas now thou shalt smite Syria but thrice" (2 Kings 13:19).

Despite the prophet's hand on his, the king's weak-willed character showed through. Joash was not bold. While obedient, his heart was not in it as he struck the arrows just three knocks on the ground—typical of a hazy temperament. A man of powerful personality would have done even that small job well, and would have smitten the ground time after time, giving it a good hammering.

God loves vigorous souls who put everything they have into what they do, however small the order. No command of God is a matter of unimportance. "Whatsoever thy hand findeth to do, do it with thy might" (Eccles. 9:10), Solomon told his young followers. What you are doesn't show just in the big battles, but in the little ones as well. You won't kill a Goliath if you run away from a bear or a lion.

God can do so much for you if you give yourself wholly to Him and to His commands. "Whatever He says to you, do it," Mary told the servants who were concerned that the wedding guests had run out of wine. No matter how foolish, no matter how irrational—just do it!

138

Consider Joseph. In Potiphar's home, in prison, or in charge of Egypt's harvests, he put everything he had into his job. That was the way he became master of Egypt. Do all you can, when you can, wherever you are, and God will make you ruler over much.

When I laid my hands on Sister C., I was shown something important. The gifts of the Spirit are not to be reserved for some future occasion, but are to be used today. With the hand of God upon you, Take up bow and arrow! Open the window! Shoot!

Part Four
Success

13
Impotent or Important?

The sign of the living Christ is an empty tomb, not an empty church. Some people think a successful church, one that attracts all manner of people, can't be spiritual. What is our vision? God with His back to the wall? God as a charitable cause? A make-do church, always threadbare, merely scraping the bottom of the barrel?

From Genesis to Revelation, no such picture is found. God's servants went to the nations and turned the tides of history. Paul caused Felix to tremble, and witnessed before the emperor Nero himself. He could say to the Roman Governor Festus, King Agrippa, Queen Bernice, and numerous high officials, "this thing was not done in a corner" (Acts 26:26). Jesus challenged the whole of Israel and its rulers, and after He had ascended, the whole world faced the same challenge.

Is your God a nonentity? Is He impotent? Or is He important and omnipotent? My God is not the God of a little ghetto of believers that nobody takes notice of. The God to serve is the great "I AM," the One who cowed Pharaoh. The Bible is a success story. The idea of a Gospel which doesn't make progress is the exact opposite to the Gospel we read of in the Word. The Bible sets before the church a plan for advance in the face of all opposition and evil.

We have seen plenty of opposition in the world. The devil reigns in some areas, I've come to know firsthand. I've come up against antagonism, false religion, crime, and sin in all forms. But the Gospel I preach has battered the devil. Multitudes beyond number have started following the conquering King Jesus. African governments have supported our CfaN Gospel crusades, and at times have even given us official police escorts from airports and to the crusade sites.

In the next chapters, I want to encourage the expectation of blessing for the work of God. Anything else would not be the Word of God. The Bible never offers us comfort for decline. God's servants are committed to triumph. Pentecost is revival.

14
Seven Steps to Success

Some have wishes. Others, like Joshua, have purposes. A whole generation of Israel wished—and died still wishing. They had a wishbone but no backbone. Joshua turned "wishes" into land, cities, homes, and possessions. Unbelieving Israel whined and died in the wilderness, while a believing Joshua wined and dined in rich Canaan, the Promised Land.

When God said "Go," even after forty years of wilderness wandering, Joshua's "go" had not gone. Within three days he went; but Israel had given up. To them, the Promised Land was a fantasy. Joshua, however, made the 450-year-old dream come true.

Once God had commissioned him, Joshua did not wait. The right moment had come. For Joshua, however, it was not a question of striking while the iron was hot, but of striking *until* the iron was hot. He did not wait for a special day. Joshua made the day an occasion. For forty years, Joshua had seen a victory waiting to happen. It happened when he decided. The door of history swung open at his touch.

There were seven factors behind his success, all outlined in chapter one of the Book of Joshua, this "Book of Success." All of the seven victory factors lay in his own heart, not in his circumstances. That is the difference between what happens for some people and what does not happen for others. Success is in ourselves, not in our circumstances.

It began with a funeral when "The Lord spake unto Joshua . . . Moses' minister, saying, Moses my servant is dead; now therefore arise, go . . . " (Josh. 1:2).

What a moment to go! The man who was supposed to lead them was dead. And the people expected God to say, "Moses my servant is dead, so you can't go now. Go back to Egypt and start over. Your beginning was wrong." Instead, He ordered, "Go"!

True, it was a disastrous hour. However, such a time is the hour for God. He revels in doing things in disastrous hours, bringing life out of death.

Moses was one of the half-dozen greatest men of all time. Brought up as a prince, he was a genius, a born leader, an organizer, a writer, a personality who carried with him the aura of God as no other man on earth. How could Joshua compare to this giant? Would Israel say, "Who does this Joshua think he is? Why, he was only Moses' servant! Joshua—lead us?"

Moses should have been the one to lead them into Canaan. How could any lesser man do it? To Joshua, the answer was that he could do what Moses did not do, because Moses already had accomplished what Joshua could never have done. Since Moses had been before him and done his mighty work, Joshua now could take the land. Moses had done everything he could. If Joshua did not take the final step over into Canaan, he would fail Moses.

Great men have gone before us all. It would be easy to feel too small to take their places. People ask, "Where are the new Pauls and Peters, the present-day Luthers and Wesleys?" But God does not want those men today. He wants us—the way He made us. Moses was made for the Sinai. Joshua was made for Canaan. The great ones of the past have made everything ready for us—for the final push before Jesus comes. We must not let them down.

Those who went before us fought for freedom, for the Bible, for truth, for the Holy Spirit. They have left us wonderful resources. We can take up where they left off. Pygmies can wave the torches of giants. It was Jesus who said those who believed in Him would do "greater works than these . . ." (John 14:12).

Christian giants did their job, and now we do ours. They did not evangelize the world, but they opened it up. Now God says, "Paul is dead; Livingstone is dead. Arise, go in and possess the land." What they could not do, we can do! Hallelujah! The vision in their hearts is the vista before our very eyes–the world for Jesus Christ. We must cast off our feelings of inferiority. We must not compare the Christians of today with the Christians of the past. A man's greatness lies only in God in any age. Joshua could do what Moses did not— because he had Moses' God.

That is the first secret: *Realize your greatness is in God.*

"With God all things are possible," Gabriel told the young virgin kneeling before him (Matt. 19:26). Note the preposition is "with." W*ith* God, not *to* God. To *you* all things are possible *with* God.

What had God said to Joshua?

"Every place that the sole of your foot shall tread upon, that have I given unto you" (Josh. 1:3).

Joshua rode into Canaan, not on the back of a huge Arabian stallion, but upon the promises of God. And God had not said it to Moses only. He had promised the land to Abraham, Isaac, Jacob, and Joseph. The people of Israel inherited the promise, but that promise was not to be fulfilled merely for the physical descendants of these great men. Only those who were the "faith" descendants of Abraham could claim the Promised Land.

One entire generation of Abraham's physical offspring died on the wrong side of the border—in unbelief. Only two men were his true children: Caleb and Joshua. The faithless all died in the wilderness. They had disinherited themselves from the covenant promise. The two faith children lived, later leading a believing second generation to conquer the land. How? They took the land by stepping on it. They were not content merely with the title deeds. They entered into their estate.

That is the second secret: *All of God's promises that were made to others become ours by faith.*

These promises are made-to-measure, tailored to our needs. They are as much for you as if God personally appeared and spoke them to you. Your only requirement is to put them on. The Lord said to Joshua, "there remaineth yet very much land to be possessed" (Josh. 13:1). And Joshua later complained to the children of Israel, "How long are ye slack to go to possess the land?" (Josh. 18:3). In fact, they didn't yet own one acre. The only land remaining to be possessed was what Joshua had made up his mind to take. It was his by faith. And remember, "Faith is the substance of things hoped for" (Heb. 11:1). Joshua had a vision, he laid claim to it, and he went ahead to get it:

> From the wilderness and this Lebanon, even unto the great river, the river Euphrates, all the land of the Hittites, and unto the great sea toward the going down of the sun, shall be your coast. (Josh. 1:4)

Today when people long for visions they seek a thrill, a supernatural experience, a mystical pleasure. That is not what God intended. God does not give visions to confirm us or to make us feel good. His visions are given to change the world. God's true dreamers are practical men, not mystics. Believing dreamers are realists; the stuff of their dreams is concrete substance. They don't stumble onto success accidentally.

Hope, one of the three great abiding Christian qualities, is created by vision. Faith makes hope feasible.

Joshua had an aim, a vision—and he was hungry for God's maximum. The Promised Land boundaries described by God had their own secret–they were expandable, encompassing anywhere from 135,000 to one million square kilometers. How? When God said "the river Euphrates," its geographical position meant that Israel could extend to any point on the river—so the border was expandable. It allowed for ever-increasing faith and ever-enlarging vision. God had given a rubber-band promise with built-in elasticity which could satisfy the spiritually boldest. Joshua's attitude was that of a man of maximum faith; he was going to take all God promised.

What an unlikely dream for Israel, a ragtag bunch of runaway slaves! But Joshua dreamed dreams. And dreamers are the folks who change the world. Joshua was no longer a youth, and he anticipated the prophecy of Joel: "Your old men shall dream dreams" (Joel 2:28). Dreams of world conquest for Christ are a charismatic feature. It was that dream which drove the people to seek the power of Pentecost at the beginning of the Pentecostal revival. That was what God sent His power to do; that was what they could not live without.

That is the third secret of success: *Get a vision of what you should do for and with God, then work to bring it about.*

Without vision, the people perish.

"As I was with Moses, so I will be with thee," God told Joshua (Josh. 1:5). One of the most deeply rooted beliefs (actually, unbeliefs) is that God is more with some people than with others. We even make all kinds of excuses by which we explain why this is so. We say some are more holy, or more prayerful, or more something. We act as if the presence of God depended upon us. But the promise of His presence is unconditional. God promised, "I will never fail thee, nor forsake thee" (Josh. 1:5). He said it to Joshua and it was repeated thirteen hundred years later in Hebrews 13:5. God is with us not because we are good or when we have great faith that He is there. No such terms are laid down. He is with us because He has committed Himself to it, irrevocably.

We are looking at the wrong sign when we try to judge whether God is with people or not. We cannot judge by what a person accomplishes or fails to accomplish. Does God shrink or swell according to whom He is with? God is not "more" with an evangelist than He is with a pastor, or more with a pastor than He is with a church member. He is not more with a big church than with a little assembly, just as he wasn't more with Moses than with Joshua.

Moses had the most extraordinary experiences with God any man ever had, and Joshua could not share these experiences fully at the time. But it was to Joshua that God said, "I will not fail thee, nor forsake thee." The presence of God with us does not vary with our callings or with our successes. If God was only with us when we had success, success would never come.

People often say, "Why does God use that particular person? I could do the same thing." Exactly! You could! So why not start now and do what the other person is doing? How can God use you if you never do what that person does? That is why He doesn't use you.

A disgruntled employee stood by his boss's desk, complaining that he earned so much less than his boss. He said, "I could be sitting where you are. I am as good an engineer as you are."

The boss replied, "That's right, you could be sitting here. Why aren't you? I started this business with nothing, and you could have done the same." But most men don't want to pay the price. They want someone to give it to them, all wrapped up without pain or hardship. Joshua knew that even though God had given him the land, there was a price to be paid to take it. And he was willing to pay that price.

That is the fourth secret of success: *Go forth knowing God is with you as much as He is with anybody. Don't hang around waiting for the right circumstances.*

God is your circumstance! He is with you. Others simply took advantage of this great circumstance, believed it, and acted on it. God proved it. Joshua's name was originally *Hoshea* (salvation), but Moses added the divine name to it, making *Jehoshua*, or, in English, Joshua. Incidentally, when that is translated into the Greek it comes out *Jesus*.

Your name, linked with God's name, means something, too. With it you can go forth in the name of the Lord with strength and courage as God ordered Joshua:

Be strong and of a good courage. (Josh. 1:6)

Only be thou strong and very courageous. (Josh.1:7)

Be strong and of a good courage; be not afraid,
neither be thou dismayed. (Josh. 1:9)

God drummed this into the soul of Joshua three times. After the first time He gave the first reason—"I will be with thee."

The second time He added "only"—"only be thou strong and very courageous."

On the third repetition He gave another reason: "Have not I commanded thee?" God commands, and that is when God commends. God gives us reasons for going forward when we find excuses for holding back—treating our fears as virtues.

We say, "I am not one to push myself." Or, "If God wants me to do it, He will put me there." Or, "We must not run in front of God." Or,

"I am waiting for a clear leading from God—we must not presume."
Or, "I am waiting for someone to pay me to do it." Or, "I do not seek
great things for myself, but I try to keep humble."

Men are dying. Are these honest or sufficient reasons? Or is our
fear holding us back? Everything the devil throws at us makes us afraid.
God, however, has given us something to counteract it. There are,
indeed, causes for our hesitation and nervousness. But they are natural–
not supernatural. God calls us to a new life of adventure and daring
in the exhilaration of the Christian life. Paul said he was not afraid to
preach the Gospel at Rome. Maybe he was nervous about it, as he
was at Corinth where he said he went "in fear and trembling." But he
did not give in to his feelings. He enjoyed the experience of God
strengthening him as he nearly single-handedly faced pagan Europe.
He understood the power of God to overcome fear. Throughout the
scriptures, we find similar words of strength and faith:

What time I am afraid—I will trust in thee. (Ps. 56:3)

The righteous are bold as a lion. (Prov. 28:1)

He spake boldly in the name of the Lord. (Acts 9:29)

Therefore abode they [Paul and Barnabas] speaking boldly in
the Lord. (Acts 14:3)

He began to speak boldly in the synagogue. (Acts 18:26)

[Paul] spake boldly for the space of three months. (Acts 19:8)

They saw the boldness of Peter and John. (Acts 4:13, NIV)

Lord . . . enable your servants to speak your word with great boldness.
(Acts 4:29)

They spake the word of God with boldness. (Acts 4:31)

These men were not super-humans who didn't know what fear
was. They felt its quivering pangs. So did Elijah, whom James said was

"subject to like passions as we are" (James 5:17). But they conquered their fears. How? They remembered God had sent them. They obeyed and threw the responsibility to Him. His reassuring question, "Have not I commanded thee?" rang in their ears. In that case, why fear man, "whose breath is in his nostrils" (Isa. 2:22)?

Paul never asked people to pray that the power of the Spirit would rest upon him. He knew it already did (Rom. 15:29). God was with him, and he knew it. He requested only this:

> That utterance may be given unto me, that I may open my mouth boldly, to make known the mystery of the gospel, For which I am an ambassador in bonds: that therein I may speak boldly, as I ought to speak. (Eph. 6:19–20)

Note the phrase "as I ought to speak." Paul was God's ambassador sent to speak.

That is the fifth secret of success: *Be bold in Christ.*

Wesley said, "I am too **afraid** of God to be afraid of men." The fear of God casts out the fear of man. Jesus said, "Be not afraid, only believe"(Mark 5:36). Literally that means "Don't have phobia, have faith." The opposite of fear is not courage, but *faith.* As one man said, "Fear knocked at the door. Faith answered. No one was there."

> Observe to do according to all the law, which Moses my servant commanded thee; turn not from it to the right hand or to the left, that thou mayest prosper withersoever thou goest.
> This book of the law shall not depart out of thy mouth; but thou shalt meditate therein day and night, that thou mayest observe to do according to all that is written therein; for then thou shalt make thy way prosperous, and then thou shalt have good success. (Josh. 1:7–9)

That word contains all the secrets of success. You can study the most erudite books about the Bible, with the finest scholarship, but "the secret of the Lord is with them that fear him" (Ps. 24:14). The hidden things of God—these are not known by the intellect. They are incommunicable. They sprout and flower in our souls as we read the Word. The Bible is not a book of cryptic mysteries. It is plain enough, but only when grasped by the hand of faith.

When Christ taught us to pray, "Give us this day our daily bread," He also meant the Word of God. Read it daily. The Father then will interpret it to us and feed our souls daily. The Bible is not for pedantics. Some want to use it to correct others; others use it to discuss phrases and words. All of those users miss the throb of God's heart.

A preacher has one task: to preach the Word, as Paul said to Titus. Preach the Word, meditate in the Word at all times ("day and night"), get your message from the Word. Say what it says. Never be selective, adjusting the Gospel to suit the public palate.

"Here may the wretched sons of want exhaustless riches find." You will never be short of ministry as long as you are full of the Word. Read it when you cannot study it. It is not the "deep things," dug up by going through a whole reference library, but the simplest statement which can set you on fire—and ignite others as well. Throughout the world, the need for Word ministry is only too apparent. Preachers with jokes, "thoughts," psychology, charming speeches, and good advice are aplenty. Some have nothing to offer except a neat homiletical arrangement, nicely alliterated with correct introduction and denouement, like a beautiful frame with no picture.

The Word makes a person a prophet, not a mere pulpit performer. Understanding of the Word is vital. Those who give themselves to teaching and preaching this Word will find multitudes of hungry people waiting, like fledglings in a nest.

Most of all, the power of God is released through the Gospel, the Word of God. Every time it is preached, it creates. It is a wonderful moment when the Holy Spirit acts, as He is bound to do. There is no need to prove Scripture; it will prove itself.

That is the sixth secret of success: *"This book of the law shall not depart out of thy mouth"*(Josh. 1:8). *If others seem to prosper without it, do not follow them. For you, here is the real way—the Word, the Word, The Word!*

"Within three days ye shall pass over this Jordan, to go in to possess the land, which the Lord your God giveth you to possess it" (Josh. 1:11). This is what I like about Joshua—he was immediate. Israel had been on the east bank of the Jordan for an entire generation. The river was not very wide, but it might as well have been the ocean. The other side was only a legend of their fathers, a Cloud-Nine golden fancy, the beautiful isle of somewhere and sometime.

Then one morning, a morning like any other, when it looked as if they would be tent dwellers forever in the wilderness, the trumpet sounded! The people were galvanized, and the gates of history swung open. The order was given, "Prepare to enter the land in three days."

How many Christian dreams and ideas have been shelved—put aside as too idealistic—for some indefinite future? God has no indefinite futures. He gives commands and promises for immediate realization. The Father knows the hour.

The revival everybody wants is now. Signs and wonders are now. Bold going forth with the Gospel is now. Opening those new churches is now.

The Israelites crossed the Jordan and looked at the key city, Jericho. As the faithless spies had essentially said, it was "Walled up to heaven, and we are as grasshoppers." There it is, that grasshopper mentality! "As he thinketh in his heart, so is he" (Prov. 23:7). If you think you are a grasshopper, you are! A man is what he believes. You are not a grasshopper in God. Never!

God said, "A dwarf . . . shall not come nigh to offer the bread of his God" (Lev. 21:20). The only dwarfs in God's sight are people little in faith, suffering from a grasshopper syndrome. The common phrase "full stature of the man" does not describe those who are unable to take the Promised Land.

The walls were there, dwarfing all of them, like the ten faithless spies had reported long before. But this time Israel was inspired. They felt big enough to blow those walls down with the blast of a trumpet. They needed no dynamite. They walked around the walls for six days while Jericho's inhabitants jeered, amused by such odd warfare. Then, down the walls went. We are big, but only in God.

That is the seventh secret of success: *Go in now to take the land.*

Israel did not just march and blow trumpets. When the walls fell, they went in, fought, and took the city. Long ago the walls of the city fell when, as Jesus said, He saw Satan fall as lightning from heaven. "Now shall the prince of this world be cast out" (John 12:31), but that is not all that has to be done. We are now commanded to go in over those fallen walls with the sword of the Word, preaching the Gospel and taking the city for God.

15
Positive Initiative

"Find your gift and use it," the experts say. If you have a gift, take that advice. Don't bury your talent in the earth. But this advice could be an excuse for some folk to settle back in their armchairs. These are the ones who say they have no gift.

The Bible has a better way. "Whatsoever thy hand findeth to do, do it with thy might" (Eccles. 9:10). In other words, get busy in God's vineyard, even if you only do a bit of weeding.

Open your eyes, take a look at the need, and get busy. In some cases, the call of God is the need. If you are looking at your talents, your known abilities, you'll probably leave most tasks to someone else. It is the call of God and what needs to be done that matters.

We should not consult with ourselves about our gifts, for by faith God can lift us beyond ourselves and our limitations. It isn't you who does the work. It's God. Without Him, you can do nothing. However, through Christ you can do all things. We can walk on the water if we're called, for all things are possible to those who believe.

What we believe, we are—even when we don't believe we are anything. Don't undersell yourself to yourself. Selling yourself short is not humility; it is denial of the very purpose for which you were born. Here is a vital principle—the call of God must be obeyed if you want the power of God to work through you.

What does God want? The first thing He wants you to do is *not* to spend years finding out what He wants you to do. God keeps no one waiting for that long. If He wants a job done, there would be no point in keeping us guessing about it. Why should He do that? It would be ridiculous to hide from you what His wishes for you are. Nor does He make it terribly difficult for you to find out.

God always has a task at hand. It may not be a great task; it may be nothing heroic. Perhaps it is a job "beneath your dignity," one that could even be considered menial. Paul sat, making tents—not planning intents. Faithful in the little things his hand found to do, God made him master of much.

Some want God to speak and guide them because they despise the day of small beginnings. They assume God has some great work for them and that it surely cannot be a little thing. "Seekest thou great things for thyself? seek them not," said Jeremiah to his secretary/ servant (Jer. 45:5). You can't steer a boat that isn't moving. God waits for you to move before He tells you which direction to take. He *does* guide. "I being in the way, the Lord led me," is the principle upon which our lives should be based. *You take the initiative for God.* That is how Paul went on those famous travels.

If there is a hole in the dam, plug it; don't pass a resolution about it. If a foe is breaking into the Promised Land, the demand is obvious: Fight him off! Don't wait! Don't ask God what to do, or study whether you have the gift of fighting off foes. One man who either did not wait when he should, or did wait when he shouldn't, was King Saul. Doing nothing because we can't do something mighty is nothing but pride.

The Worst of Times Is the Best of Times

For centuries there was competition between Israel and the Philistines for the land of Israel. The Philistines were the traditional enemies to Israel, both physically and spiritually. We can compare spiritual principles in their history to Christian work and warfare today. Constant Israeli-Philistine skirmishes took place until David finally subdued the Philistines.

After Saul became king, he created a standing army of three thousand men, placing a third of them under his son Jonathan. At that time the Philistines had the upper hand. They put garrisons here and there throughout the land of Israel, including one in the strategic pass from Bethel to Jericho, where the town of Michmash stood.

Jonathan already had made an attack on the Philistine forces at this time, so the Philistines had placed a good army in Michmash. In readiness, King Saul placed about six hundred men on the other side of the pass, at Gibeah. He was all set for war.

But Saul didn't attack. He only waited. His finger was on the trigger, but he refused to open fire. The enemy sat comfortably in Israel, occupying and exploiting the land that God had given to the Israelis—the land that their forefathers had taken at great expense. It was a phony war; nobody did anything.

Jonathan, Saul's son, was much like David. They were soul mates with a similar, restless temperament of do-or-die. Jonathan became impatient just sitting, fingering the blades of grass with one elbow on the ground. He thought of his father who "tarried under a pomegranate tree," keeping cool. Eventually, saying nothing to his father, Jonathan and his armor bearer decided to take action themselves—just the two of them. The enemy was there; why leave them unmolested? They would settle down in the land forever if something wasn't done.

Two Daring Disciples

The only passage to the small Philistine garrison above them led through a defile, a narrow canyon which at one point passed between two sharp rocks. Jonathan not only would have to climb up, which gave the defenders an advantage against him, but he also would have to get through that narrow defensive position. One Philistine could hold off an army there, like Horatius did at the Tiber bridge. So Jonathan said to his shield bearer, "It may be that the Lord will work for us: for there is no restraint to the Lord to save by many or by few" (1 Sam. 14:6).

It was a venture of faith. They knew the Lord could save Israel using only the two of them. However, if everybody simply sat in the shade under the pomegranate trees, no one would be saved. That kind of inaction meant the occupying enemy would be there forever. Some Israeli action was needed if the Philistines were to be driven out. It didn't matter to God whether it was done officially or by personal initiative.

So the two young men decided on a test. They would come out of hiding and stand where the Philistines could see them. If their enemies said, "Come up to us and we'll teach you a lesson" (1 Sam. 14:12, NIV), Jonathan and his armor bearer would do just that. The Philistines never would have believed that they would attempt such a foolhardy escapade—two young Israeli warriors taunting twenty soldiers in the commanding position above them.

Jonathan's "test" was actually an act of faith. He proposed to do something very courageous. His "fleece" was that the Philistines would challenge him if he made himself conspicuous, something his enemies would surely do. Some people put out "fleeces" which are absurd; they take guidance from conditions which are either too easy or too hard. These are those who usually get fleeced by the devil in the end.

The Philistines did see Jonathan, and said exactly what Jonathan expected—"Come up here." They weren't exactly spoiling for battle at the time. They, too, were enjoying lounging around their command post. Besides, they didn't believe the two young Israeli soldiers would attempt anything so foolhardy. So they turned their backs and carried on, doing nothing in particular.

But, in faith, Jonathan and his armor bearer did what was considered venturesome to attempt. The pair of them went up, creeping forward on hands and knees. They sneaked through the wadi and past the narrow passage with the outcropping of rocks. Actually, the Philistines were sure they had scared them off. Therefore they were not prepared when the two men sprang their attack on the astonished garrison. Jonathan's faith gave him a sheer audacity which won the day.

Meanwhile, Saul was spending his time talking to a priest of the Lord, probably seeking help and guidance when it was obvious what his real duty was. He hoped God would do something (1 Sam. 14:3), not understanding the principle that God was waiting on someone who believed in Him to act on faith.

God, in fact, *did* do something. He did it when Jonathan went into action. To begin with, the Lord helped their valor. Then He rose in

His might and did His own thing. He brought about an earth tremor, not uncommon in that area.

The outcome was panic. It spread throughout the enemy lines. The Philistine force became confused. Rumors flew and the soldiers fled. Jonathan's father, King Saul, heard the commotion. Reports came the Philistines were fleeing. He found courage and led his men into the melee, giving chase. Israeli prisoners, whom the Philistines were holding, took heart and turned on their captors. Israeli civilians, who had hidden themselves among the rocks of Mount Ephraim, too frightened before to fight, now became bold and threw their weight into the rout of the enemy. Trapped, the Philistines suffered a severe defeat.

Ordinary Day

All this happened on just an ordinary day. The historian makes a special note in the record: "Now it came to pass upon a day." That means it was no special day. It was a day without divine leadings and revelations. It was an unpromising day without auspicious signs. The conditions were bad. The victory occurred because Jonathan simply made up his mind to fight. He made that day special himself. God's day coincided exactly with the day Jonathan decided they had hung around long enough.

The king had been waiting for something to happen, perhaps waiting to be pushed into action. Overly cautious, he was hoping God would make the first move, which was why he talked to the priest. Jonathan couldn't hang around for eventualities and signs, for some kind of "super-spiritual leading". He consulted no priest. His "fleece" was almost sure to put him into battle. He simply did with all his might what his hand found to do.

God has a thousand-year calender with only one day on it. It is marked "TODAY." Jesus Himself challenged those who talked about waiting for harvest; He said the harvest is ripe now. The prophet Haggai launched a blistering attack on people in Jerusalem once when they said, "The time is not come, the time that the Lord's house should be built" (Hag. 1:2). It was a cheap excuse. They were more interested in building their own houses than the house of God.

Revival Initiative

Over and over I hear people say the same thing: "The time isn't right." They act as if weather or circumstances or lack of money can thwart the power of God! Revival isn't for when there already *is* revival, but for when there isn't a sign of it. Revivals always begin when nothing is happening, when there are no signs of God's moving and nothing encouraging looms on the horizon. Precisely *because* things were bad all around, bold men of faith went out to change them. If we wait until the situation is better, we shall never go at all. In fact, what's the point then? Jonathan struck when a victory seemed impossible, and that is why he succeeded. God delighted to join in and prove His power.

We are all praying for a mighty revival to sweep America, Europe, and the rest of the world. Pray, pray on! But don't wait until it comes and Gospel preaching becomes easy. We need to get on with what we can do now. We can win thousands for Christ while waiting for revival. And not only that . . . such action could be the start of revival. It is true that revival is "a sovereign act of God." But it is equally true that revival can be caused as men of God act in faith.

This was the principle which guided those first-century Christians: "And they went forth, and preached every where, the Lord working with them, and confirming the word with signs following" (Mark 16:20).

Those blessed people didn't sit and wait for the Lord to go forth, as so many do today. "*They* went forth." In other words, they took the initiative and the Lord gladly obliged! I am fully persuaded that God allows us to pull the trigger for mighty outpourings of His Holy Spirit. By His grace, I have witnessed it numerous times! We need Holy-Ghost initiative! Revival takes anointed men and women of God who exercise the audacity of faith!

When Jonathan and his armor bearer went up, by their own initiative, for a private skirmish with the enemy on their hands and knees, they accomplished a far bigger victory than they thought possible. It forces us to ask: Is God waiting for me? Am I His Jonathan?

Anybody can believe God when God already is moving. Real faith comes into play when God doesn't seem to be acting. God loves the man and the woman who gamble upon His help! This is the formula for triumph, blessing, and revival. How many more people can you think of who did exactly that? Anybody who ever achieved anything new for God did it this way—by stepping out in faith. These are the ones who dared do something when no one else thought it was the right time. Every revival in history has started that way.

One minister longed for God's greater movings—to see the Lord heal the afflicted and work miracles. When he approached an older minister, he was told, "God will do those things when revival comes. So wait." That's what the religious leaders told Jesus when He announced the beginning of His public ministry in Nazareth. The unfriendly congregation was putting off, indefinitely, what God promised He would do. But Jesus declared, "This day is this scripture fulfilled in your ears" (Luke 4:21). And this was in a town like Nazareth, with its bad reputation! How much revival atmosphere could there be in a synagogue where a man was there with a withered hand, and all the cynics were watching, hoping to accuse Jesus of healing on the Sabbath? The conditions were hardly propitious. But Jesus healed the man—*because* the time is ripe when the need is greatest.

That time is today.

Who is God waiting for?

Could it be you?

What are *you* waiting for?

16

No Bargains with the Devil

From time to time, I have been invited to join a television panel to discuss religious issues. The participants generally meet just before going on the air. On one occasion none of us knew each other, and we had to be introduced. There was a short time in which to chat with one another before the program began. Following introductions there was a time for small talk before going out to face the cameras. Conversation got around to horse racing, as it was the time of the July Handicap. One of the men professed to be an atheist, but he seemed to have the names of all the horses and jockeys at his fingertips. Since I had no knowledge of horse racing and betting, I just sat quietly—occupying the time with silent prayer.

As I began to pray, asking the Lord to guide me in the discussion that was to follow, the others continued to discuss horses and gambling. Suddenly something flashed through my spirit. Turning to the race-horse expert, I said, "Let tell you something about horses."

The atheist was immediately interested. I said, "I have put all my money on the white horse in the Book of Revelation."

Perhaps he thought that I was an authority and just had been silent on the subject. He looked baffled. "White horse in the Book of Revelation?" he asked.

That seemed to be the only horse that particular horse expert had never heard of. "Who's the rider on the white horse?" he asked.

Inside, I felt glad. His question was exactly the one I had wanted. Of course he was asking for the name of the jockey. Instead I said, "in Revelation, chapter 19, it says that the rider's name is 'Faithful and True . . . The Word of God; He is the Son of God, Jesus Christ.'"

The man looked mystified. I continued, "Mister, I have not put just my money on Him. As a matter of fact, I have no money. I have put my life and my soul on Him. He's the One I back with everything I've got, and I know I am going to win!"

Although the atheist was uncomfortable with my obvious reference to Jesus as my Savior, nevertheless he continued to talk long after the program was over. He left the studio, still uncommitted, but at least he was forced to think about the claim of God on his life.

That is where the race starts for us, with the finish "a dead cert," in racing terms. For us, the end is a living certainty. It is the assurance of Jesus as the eternal and universal winner. Knowledge like that is bound to have a tremendous effect upon our everyday lives.

The Uncursable Winner

Do you know, with absolute assurance, that you have joined the winning side? Then you will not be harassed by fear. There is no way a believer can be cursed to lose. He is uncursable. He has the winner, God Himself, on his side. "If God be for us, who can be against us?" (Rom. 8:31).

Fear is forged in hell. It is issued by Satan as a standard weapon to all demons. Demons know the meaning of fear, for they are full of fear themselves, like scorpions are full of poison. They know its paralyzing force. Fear is Satan's venom. He wants to sting us all, making us sick with fear. The devil will create a future for us packed with fears. But such fears are illusions—mere phantoms. They only will take on substance if we accept them. We must exorcise these ghosts.

Fear is the first thing to be rid of. The evil one will surround evangelism with a cloud of misgiving. Conquering dread is the blow which neutralizes the enemy's primary attack. God promises: "No weapon that is formed against thee shall prosper" (Isa. 54:17). We have our own weapon, the Word of God, the sword of the Spirit (Eph. 6:17). Wielding this mighty sword means we're no longer at the mercy of the enemy.

A good example is the story in Numbers 22–24 of Balak's plot to curse Israel. The Israelites were on the march from Kadesh-barnea in the Sinai toward the Promised Land. The cloud of God's anointing was moving and they were under it. They had crushed every enemy army that had risen up before them and were now moving north along the eastern ridge of the Aravah, through the present kingdom of Jordan, in the land of the ancient Moabites. As they approached the Jordan River, where it empties into the Dead Sea, they camped on the eastern shore of the Jordan near the city of Jericho. Balak, the prince of Moab, was desperate to defeat the forces of Israel. Realizing he could not do it through military might, he tried another approach. He offered Balaam, a prophet, money to curse Israel.

Balaam was not unwilling. He loved money. He knew the Lord was blessing Israel, but he decided to prostitute himself to Balak, just to get his money, and agreed to put a curse on Israel. But before he did, he sought the Lord—hoping God would give him some kind of prophecy.

It was a strange situation. We find the heathen Balak and the prophet Balaam, who knew about God but didn't know Him personally, clambering up the rocky peaks of the "high places of Baal." There they built seven altars and offered seven bulls and rams in sacrifice. Perhaps, they hoped, some dark, occultic force would join them– blighting the progress of God's people. But God does not deal in curses against His own people. Balaam and Balak persisted, trying hard from every angle, but their attempt was futile. They looked at the tents of Israel at the foot of the high hills. In the midst of the camp was the tabernacle, with the glory cloud of God's presence, the very banner of the Lord, constantly there. "He that keepeth Israel shall neither slumber nor sleep" (Ps. 121:4). Israel was resting there early in the morning, safe beneath the outspread wings of Jehovah, which were invisible to Israel's enemies.

Balaam and Balak did their worst on the top of the mountain. Raging, they worked to cast a spell of misfortune over the Israelites. But God's people slept on peacefully. When Balaam opened his mouth to curse, his words came forth as blessings instead. The tribes were there, unaware and undisturbed. The Israelites were relaxing their heads on the pillow of His promises, safe under His divine protection.

The attempt to turn dark forces against Israel only succeeded in making the two plotters look ridiculous. The Bible concludes the episode with a touch of quiet mockery. "And Balaam rose up, and went and returned to his place, and Balak also went his way." That's all that happened!

When Balak chided Balaam for not cursing Israel, as he had earlier agreed, the prophet answered:

> How shall I curse, whom God hath not cursed? Or how shall I defy, whom the Lord hath not defied?
> The Lord his God is with him and the shout of a king is among them. (Num. 23:8, 21)

Frightening Satan

Fear plays into the hands of the devil. He can do no real damage, except to make us fear. The devil is a con artist. When Balaam was forced to speak the truth, he wound up showing us that God's people are not cursable. We are immune because we have been redeemed. What was true of God's redeemed people then, is true of the redeemed today. Fear hears the shout of Goliath, but faith hears the shout of the King of kings.

> There is no enchantment against Jacob, neither is there any divination against Israel: according to this time it shall be said of Jacob and of Israel, What hath God wrought! (Num. 23:23)

Just a few years before this happened with Balak and Baalam, the howling winds of death had been heard across Egypt. Yet no Israeli home knew its cold breath. The blood of the lamb of the passover marked every household, making it safe from the curse of death. Jehovah, on hovering wings, protected them from the avenging angel. Every child of God today is covered and marked by the blood of Jesus. Each one of us is beyond the reach of the powers of hell, of witches, of spells, of curses, of demons, or of all the devil's minions. Principalities and powers in heavenly places cannot touch us while we rest beneath the banner of the precious blood of the Savior, our Passover Lamb. That protection is impenetrable and invulnerable.

The man who fears is the devil's ally—whether he likes it or not. Fear is an infection, a sickness. It can spread among Christians. The reason God prohibited the children of Israel from talking while marching around the walls of Jericho is they would have spread doubt and fear among themselves. The devil does not fear the man who fears. He knows that person is harmless. But Satan trembles when we do not fear.

When considering this I like to read the story of Nehemiah, who restored the walls around Jerusalem following his return from exile in Babylon. Some urged him to hide from the threats of his enemies. I like his reply: "Should such a man as I flee? and who is there, that, being as I am, would go into the temple to save his life? I will not go in" (Neh. 6:11). Are the people of God, the blood-bought sons and daughters of the kingdom, such people as we are, to give way to bluster and threats? God's people are not given "the spirit of fear; but of power, and of love, and of a sound mind" (2 Tim. 1:7).

Should Christians flee? *Never!*

Far from fearing, we can rejoice. "Behold, I give unto you power to tread on serpents and scorpions, and over all the power of the enemy; and nothing shall by any means hurt you" (Luke 10:19). Christians are not the hunted, but the hunters; not the attacked, but the attackers. We are not besieged. We do not have our backs to the wall. Far from it! We are God's storm troops, sent to release the hostages of hell. We are the invading forces of the Lord!

Over and over Jesus said, "Fear not!" But that was not all. He was the supreme Psychologist. Notice what He said in John 8:50: "Fear not: believe only." It was always more than just, "Don't be afraid," or "Take courage, be brave." That alone would be useless advice. Fear is a force and must be met by an equal force.

Fear is the negative force. Its sign is a minus. Somebody once told me, "Fear is the darkroom in which people develop their negatives." Only a positive force can cancel a negative one. That positive force is faith. So Jesus always said, "Fear not: believe only."

Remember: The opposite of fear is not courage, but faith.

Faith is a multipurpose weapon. It is not presumption or bravado. Remember the sons of Sceva who tried to take on demons without faith in Jesus. They almost lost their lives. A trembling saint makes a triumphant Satan; but faith frightens the foe. We are not called to tremble, but to exercise authority and to shake hell. Benaiah "plucked the spear out of the Egyptian's hand, and slew him with his own spear" (2 Sam. 23:21). So we will snatch fear from the hands of the enemy, use its own weapon, and make devils tremble.

Prince of the Power of the Air

During one of our Gospel crusades in Africa, I had an experience which gave me a new understanding of God. We were planning to use our big tent in a place called Green Valley in Transvaal. With great anticipation, I counted the hours to the first meeting. Then the tent manager phoned. They were ready to pitch the canvas tabernacle, which would hold ten thousand people, African style. But there was a problem, he said: "The ground is too soft. If we go ahead and raise the tent and the wind and rain come, the anchors and masts will lose their grip. The tent will collapse. The wet soil simply won't support it."

We were faced with a tough decision. Should we go ahead and pitch the tent, despite the weather conditions? My mind was working fast on this question. It would be a terrible thing if it all went wrong. I prayed to the Lord in my heart while I thought. Then a wonderful, divine assurance flooded my mind. "Go ahead," I told my tent manager. "In the name of Jesus, it is not going to rain or storm." And so, on that instruction, the tent went up.

We had a wonderful start. Night after night the tent was packed with people hungry for the Word of God. Then one afternoon, while I was kneeling in prayer in my van parked near the tent, I looked up and saw a mighty thunderstorm filling the western sky and heading in our direction.

There are few things as awesome as an African storm, filling the air with water. The clouds, like masses of pitch-black curly hair, were being tossed by the storm within them. *Here comes your catastrophe,* something said inside me. But then I heard the voice of the Holy Spirit answering that fear, telling me what to do: *Go and rebuke the devil!*

I went out and walked aggressively in the direction of the imminent storm. Lifting my finger and pointing, I said, "Devil, I want to talk to you in the name of Jesus. If you destroy this tent of mine, I am going to trust God for a tent three times this size!"

I looked, and at that moment, something incredible happened— the clouds parted. They began to make a detour away from and around the tent. The menace was over! The clouds and rain never reached us, and the tent stood firm for the rest of the Gospel campaign. How great is our God!

Then this wonderful truth hit me, harder than any thunderbolt which that storm may have hurled at us. *Faith frightens Satan!* My faith had scared off the devil. He probably had enough to worry about already with this tent of ours, and faith for a bigger one shook him.

"Devils . . . tremble" (James 2:19), the Bible declares. When we arise with living faith and tackle the opposition in God's strength, our faith terrorizes the arch-terrorist, the devil. "Resist the devil, and he will flee from you" (James 4:7). This is no mere untried hypothesis. John could testify, "I write unto you, young men, because ye have overcome the wicked one" (1 John 2:13). With faith in God, even "the lame take the prey" (Isa. 33:23).

My tent episode was not quite over, for something unsettling nagged at my heart. *What if the devil misunderstood my words?* I wondered. The thought kept coming back to me. So I decided to make the issue clear. I spoke to the devil in the name of Jesus once more, telling him, "I make no bargains with you. Just because you withdrew the wind and the rain does not mean I made an agreement with you about not having a bigger tent. The bigger tent comes anyway."

We are not to negotiate with the devil—we are to cast him out. That is all the Word of God tells us. Keep repeating to yourself, over and over: faith frightens Satan, faith frightens Satan, faith frightens Satan. This truth will change you from negative to positive. In Jesus, you are the victor, not the victim. Satan is the victim, because Jesus crushed the serpent's head.

The Fearless Christian

God's children can be bold. Let the Word tell you so. "By faith Moses, when he was born, was hid three months of his parents, because they saw he was a proper child; and they were not afraid of the king's commandment" (Heb. 11:23). Think of what that involved. The Egyptian state and Pharaoh, its head, had made it illegal to keep a male Hebrew baby. The law stated such children were to be killed at birth. Soldiers moved around to carry out this order. What terror and grief there must have been!

Then Moses was born. Amram and Jochebed looked upon their lovely son. They knew they could not allow the Egyptian soldiers to come into their little home and slit his throat with their knives. They decided to defy the law and hide the baby. "By faith . . . they were not afraid." Officers of the law were everywhere. Their footsteps were heard at their door, seeking the child's life. But it was not just the child's life at stake. By defying the law, they too could be killed. Yet "they were not afraid" (Heb. 11:23). Why not? Were they unnatural, unfeeling? No, they were just good parents who believed God would take care of them.

True, the situation looked impossible. Their faith seemed naive and foolish. But that's exactly the kind of situation where God works best. When things are impossible, faith is the answer. Faith is not just for the possible—that is not faith at all. The mightiest resource in the universe is the arm of God. Some can only believe God when it is for something "reasonable," something which can be managed. But, as Paul wrote, we "have no confidence in the flesh" (Phil. 3:3), that is, in our own schemes.

My African friends love to remind me of the story of the elephant and the ant. An elephant crossed a shaky bridge, and a tiny ant sat on the elephant, just behind the huge animal's ear. The bridge shook as they crossed and the ant hung on for dear life. When they were safely on the other side, the ant stood up on its hind legs and said to the elephant, "Well, *we* certainly made that bridge swing all right, didn't *we?*"

This is the kind of relationship we have with God when we rest on Him. He carries us. He makes the bridge swing. He puts His weight

172

behind us, beneath us, and at our side. It is He who builds our homes, our churches, our businesses. It is the Lord who leads us safely through life and takes us to the peak of success. How foolish for us to take any of the credit. In Him, we find the impossible possible.

Even to your old age and gray hairs I am he, I am he who
will sustain you. I have made you and I will carry you; I
will sustain you and I will rescue you. (Isa. 46:4, NIV)

Hallelujah!

The Watershed

Faith makes the difference. Faith is the mark of distinction between the believer and the non-believer. The entire world stands on one side or the other of the faith line. There are only two really different types of people—not the rich and the poor, not the black and the white, not the learned and the unlearned, not Jew and Greek, not male and female. None of these distinctions exists in Christ. God sees only believer and unbeliever. "He that believeth . . . shall be saved; but he that believeth not shall be damned" (Mark 16:16).

Faith is of the new order. Unbelief is of the old and dying order. Faith is the dividing line which runs through mankind. Either you have faith or you have no faith at all; these are the alternatives for our approach to life.

Fear sees just what man sees. Faith sees what God sees—and acts upon it. Faith creates action, and people of action: like Amram and Jochebed, the parents of Moses, like Caleb and Joshua, like the apostle Paul. Unbelief keeps us tied down in a spiritual wilderness—like Israel was for so many years. Fear and doubt magnify the difficulties, making us think people cannot be won for Christ and that the world is too strong. Without faith, we fear failure and mockery. Faith says people can be won, and so the joy of expectation grips us instead. By faith we move from minimum to maximum.

The Man Who Lived Tomorrow

Nearly all the dead in Egypt were preserved for entombment by one of two widely used mummification processes. The pharaohs were entombed in massive mausoleums, multiple coffins, and sometimes even in permanent pyramids. Those dead people were very dead! But one of them had no intention of having "R.I.P." (Rest In Peace) on his grave in Egypt. The mummy of Joseph was intended for export—the only one that ever was. Joseph knew the promises of God and what the future would hold, and he was determined not to be left out of it. Joseph, who died at the age of 110, wouldn't even be found dead in Egypt. He was the man who lived tomorrow.

"By faith Joseph . . . gave commandment concerning his bones" (Heb. 11:22). He didn't want to lie quietly in the grave when the Red Sea and the River Jordan opened. His eye of faith saw the faithfulness of God fulfilling His Word, the Word which He had given to Abraham, Isaac, and Jacob long before. In fact hundreds of years before it happened, Joseph had shouted with the armies of men who, yet to be born, would bring down the walls of Jericho. Faith renews our youth. A man of faith at the age of 110 years is younger than a critical teen-ager. So many of our young are "old" and futureless, without God and without hope. Where are the men of Joseph's battalion today? They are the defeated rabble whose song is that of the Beatles:

Yesterday, all my troubles seemed so far away . . .
I believe in yesterday.

Joseph believed, by faith, that God would go into action one day. He determined not to be left out—dead or alive. Faith gives life to the dead. It gives life to the fearful. Faith mocks at the king of terror and death. It terrifies him who has the power of death, even the devil. It gives us the power to sing with Paul as he thought of the marvelous victory already won: "O death, where is thy sting? O grave, where is thy victory?" (1 Corinthians 15:55).

174

Part Five
In Practice

17
The Trap

God underwrites His own schemes. He will supply, but we must know what His supplies are for. The Lord runs His business on cash, not credit. All we need to know is what He plans to do. Find out what God is engaged in, and throw your lot in with Him. Join the firm! Then we are authorized to requisition by faith what we need from His vast stores. We can ask God to provide for what we are doing, as long as we are doing what He does.

And what *is* God doing? He is the Savior, the God of salvation. "I, even I, am the Lord; and beside me there is no saviour" (Isa. 43:11). Salvation is not just an evangelist's pet subject, it is the Lord's "great work." God specializes in salvation. As medicine to a doctor, as music to a musician, so is the work of salvation to God. Jesus came "to seek and to save that which was lost" (Luke 19:10); and to bring "many sons unto glory" (Heb. 2:10). That's the business of God.

Now the exciting thing is we are invited to work with Him. We don't have to do this on our own, however. We don't buy a franchise and then become responsible for our own business as long as we make regular payments to the headquarters. The Gospel is God's business from start to finish—His monopoly, if you like. We can't set up Gospel shops and sell our own brand of Christianity. Jesus Christ is the Head of all the salvation work in the world. We can labor in company with Him (and it must be done at all costs) but He is still the boss. And—praise God—He pays the bills.

A friend of mine said, "If God is not the engine, I don't even want to give a push."

I added, "But if God is the engine, I don't mind being the caboose." Move with God, and nothing can stop you. Nothing can go wrong with His plans. They don't fail or derail. What God wants to live cannot and will not die.

In some cases, church projects are surviving only under intensive care. They need artificial life-support systems to keep on breathing. Such projects have little to do with God's plans. His life is not in them. When we come on these programs we need to switch off the life-support machine—pull the plug, so to speak. If real life is there, the programs will not need heart-lung equipment. What God wants to die—let die, and do not give artificial respiration. "Let the dead bury their dead," Jesus told His complaining disciples (Luke 10:60). Why maintain unproductive church machinery and expect God to pay the bills? He won't. The real business of the church is winning people for Christ.

Wrongfully and Rightfully Careful

When it comes to evangelism I've heard people say, "We must be careful with God's money"—as if God were a bit short of cash. It might be a sincere argument, but it looks suspiciously mean. Why hoard God's money in the bank? A church may save its money in case of an emergency, in order to have something for a rainy day, or it can trust God to look after any necessity that comes. The most specific and urgent of emergencies already *has* come—the need to save the dying world.

When was God "careful," calculating every penny? Was He "careful" when He made the trillions of stars and planets, where not a soul lives? Was He "careful" when He sent His own Son—stripping heaven of its wealth and parting with its greatest treasure, the Only Begotten. He beggared Himself of all He loved and all He had for the salvation of our souls. "If God spared not His own Son, but delivered Him up for us all, how shall He not with Him freely give us all things?" (Rom. 8:32).

We have an extravagant God! We are to be like Him in all things.

God's Money Plan

The Lord fills our pockets for soul-saving. When we empty them, there will be more. God's money plan is simple. "Give, and it shall be given unto you"(Luke 6:38). Give, then you will have more to give more. God spares neither Himself nor dollars (nor marks, nor pounds, nor francs) to find lost men and women. A church can't afford to save money at the expense of saving souls. Spend to save! But spend it on soul-winning projects. People will give to a live project, but not to a dead bank account. When the collection takes longer than the preaching, something is wrong. The evangelism report should come before the treasurer's report. The truth is, evangelism does not appear on the agenda at all in thousands of church business sessions. The bank statement produces more discussion than the conversion figures of the month. The church that gives, prospers. Evangelism and support of missions is essential for the health of a church. That has been proven too often to be doubted.

Tents and Intents

God guides, then provides. He leads, then feeds. That is His rule. An illustration is found with Israel. In the wilderness, manna fell where the pillar of cloud and fire was—and there only. If Israel missed staying under the cloud, they missed breakfast, lunch, and dinner. There is always enough if we are in the spot where He tells us to be.

When we were building our thirty-four-thousand-seat tent in Africa, we were in dire need of finances. The Lord had told me not to take a bank loan, and His instructions are holy to me. Ringing in my ears were the words, "Mine are the silver and gold." Then one day, a very large sum arrived—just what we needed. I hardly could believe my eyes, but not because my faith was small. It was because of where the gift was from. The donor was a lady who, in the past, had sent us a couple of dollars a month. Then, suddenly, she mailed this large gift!

This was something I felt I had to know about. I visited her to find out what had prompted her to send this amount. What she told me was almost too exciting to put into words. She said that in the middle of the night she had received a telephone call. The voice had given her an instruction to send this particular amount of money to us.

"But," she insisted, "the call was not from a human being. It was an angel of the Lord who spoke to me. I know that, because the glory of the Lord filled my room. I knew that God had given me a clear instruction. So I did just what He told me."

Well, I thought, if God put an angel in charge of our finances, it was needless for me to lie awake at night and worry. I could go to sleep and simply leave God in charge. After all, He is senior partner and reserves the right to make all decisions and raise all the money.

Donkeys

Although the Lord told me not to take out a bank loan, that does not mean all bank loans are wrong. We should not condemn those who are led differently from ourselves. God provided manna from the skies, but He has other ways also. Jesus Himself used different methods. Let us look at one of them.

When Jesus was preparing for His "triumphal entry" into Jerusalem, He needed an animal to ride upon. Leaving the Mount of Olives just outside the old city walls, He sent two of His disciples ahead of Him.

> Go ye into the village over against you; in the which at your entering ye shall find a colt tied, whereon yet never man sat: loose him, and bring him hither.
> And if any man ask you, Why do ye loose him? thus shall ye say unto him, Because the Lord hath need of him. (Luke 19:30–31)

In Matthew's account we read that Jesus also had a colt with the donkey. Jesus did not call a prayer meeting to pray to get these animals, then wait for somebody to bring them. In this case He took the initiative. "Go ye into the village . . . loose him, and bring him . . . . The Lord hath need of him."

The Lord was the One who had created all the donkeys. Why did He have to ask for one? The story tells me the Lord has needs which

He gives us the privilege of fulfilling. What if the disciples had not obeyed Jesus, but had simply sat on rocks and waited for a donkey to come wandering by? What if the man who owned the donkey had not turned over the halter rope to those who came in the name of the Lord? Surely God would have provided, but those who disobeyed would have missed the greatest of all blessings.

"The Lord hath need. . . . " His work has needs which you, and I, and all God's children can supply. It is God's wonderful arrangement to give us the joy of sharing with Him in what He does. This ought to make us happy. I imagine that later the owner of the donkeys, after he understood, must have thanked the Lord all his life for this privilege. Even the little donkey had its day. He had helped Jesus a mile or two along His way to triumph.

The Bible notes the man had "securely tightened" his donkey. It was his property, and he didn't want to lose it. The Lord said to His disciples, "loose it." Let's untie our donkeys for Jesus! We should loose our donkeys now, or we may lose them in the end. In the same way, Jesus taught that we should not hold tightly to our money.

> *We lose what on ourselves we spend,*
> *We have as treasure without end*
> *Whatever Lord to Thee we lend*
> *Who givest all.*

It is, of course, biblical to take up offerings to do what God wants done. God loves a cheerful giver, because He is one Himself. Nobody can evangelize the world alone. We all have gifts to contribute: money, talents, time, or ourselves. Only the total contribution of all of us can accomplish the task. *Together* is the only way it can be done. Not an idle hand, for the laborers are so few, and not an idle dollar or pound, for the needs are so many.

The Money Trap

Money can be a booby trap for the unwary. We need pure hearts, pure motives, and God's anointing upon our eyes to perceive the snares of the devil. I had hardly started to reach out to Africa when the Lord sent me a kind of qualifying test. A lady phoned and invited me to her house. When I arrived, I found a home that spoke of great wealth. It was beautiful and opulent.

"I wanted to meet you so much," she said, greeting me with a warm smile. "I have watched you for some time."

She soon came to the point, and it was so wildly beyond my imagination that I could only stare. She said, "I want to finance your Gospel crusades in Africa."

I almost forgot to breathe. On the table was a file, which she pushed across to me. It contained documents setting out her assets. I read, and it was as if I had discovered the Valley of Eldorado.

"You can see what I have," she said. "Iron-ore deposits, a diamond mine, et cetera." It was like meeting Croesus. "Now," she explained, "I want to form a trust and give half my assets to the work of God. Would you like to join the trustees? All this money is to be used in the service of the Lord. Will you accept it?"

Surely God was behind such liberality? Yet I heard no echo of pleasure from heaven. Instead, I felt a strange caution, though I tried to hide my lack of enthusiasm. All I could say was, "Thank you! But this is a great responsibility. I need to pray about it before committing myself."

After I got home I shared all this with my wife, Anni. She confirmed my misgivings. Neither of us had any excitement. Instead, all we felt was deep anxiety. We knew we must get down before the Lord and ask for His guidance. We prayed together: "Lord, if this is a trap of the devil, we'll have nothing to do with it."

Weeks passed. I was totally occupied with the work of our crusades. I could not bring myself to say either yes or no to the lady's offer. One night I had a fearful nightmare which I could not forget. I dreamed I stood on a river bank at dusk. The water was low, leaving only puddles and mud. A small man passed me and walked down the embankment. He beckoned me, and I followed. When I reached the middle of this almost dry river, suddenly, with an awful roar, a huge hippopotamus arose in front of me. There are two species, and this was the biggest one. I backed away from its engulfing jaws, but there was another of the monsters looming behind me. Others arose from the mud. I was surrounded on all sides. In peril and despair, I cried out, "Jesus, help me!" In my dream He did help. I woke up, but the impression of pending danger stayed with me.

While that nightmare was still on my mind, the lady contacted me again and pressed me to meet her. She wanted my decision about setting up the trust. We went, and she welcomed us again with a smile.

"Before we go into the house," she said, "let me show you around here." So we walked around her property with her. Her grounds ended at a river. We stood looking across it.

All at once, a shock went through me—as if I had been struck by lightning. That river! It was the same one I had seen in my nightmare. The river was identical, only now I was not dreaming. There was a peril lurking here. That was what the dream meant. I felt the Lord near and I was sure my answer was coming. I turned and asked the lady if we could go into the house and have prayer together.

As soon as we knelt, I heard the voice of the Lord not once, but three times. "My son, have nothing to do with this."

When we rose, I went to the wealthy lady and said, "I must decline your great generosity. Give your millions to someone else. God does not want me to have this money."

At that moment a great weight seemed to lift from my spirit. It seemed so strange. We were just beginning our work in Africa. We had great financial needs. But God showed me something in that moment. By His Spirit, He showed me my true assets were the promises in His Word. "My God shall supply all your need according to his riches in glory" (Phil. 4:19). I realized I could exhaust the millions the lady was offering, and when they were finished, my ministry would be finished also, for I would have forgotten how to rely on God.

Promissory Note

God did not want me to have a trust fund as a source of supply. He had His own trust. I must do the trusting. In fact, God had planned an even greater source than this lady's fund. I had the divine promissory note—His inexhaustible riches, backed by His own guarantees. *El Shaddai*—the God who supplies!

I've never regretted my decision, for I have been more blessed by His precious promises than by all the gold and diamonds in the world. Somehow I felt as if I had just passed a very difficult test and had progressed in the school of the Holy Spirit. I had learned that, for as long as I continued to preach the Gospel, regardless of how much it cost, the Lord would see that the bills were met. What God orders to be done, He pays for, and, if necessary, He will move heaven and earth to do it.

Giving Royally

I've quoted Philippians 4:19, "But my God shall supply all your need according to his riches in glory by Christ Jesus." The phrase "according to" (from the Greek word *kata*) means "by the standard of." That is, by the standard of His riches, not the standard of our poverty. He fills our empty sack, but does not measure it first. He gives as a king does, "running over," not as someone of modest means would be able to give. Don't ask, "Lord, can you manage to send me $9.50, please?" You might be able to get by with that, but that will not meet your need. Tell Him your real need! Let Him supply—He has a big hand.

His guests don't sit down to dry crusts; He is the Producer of all the fruit of the field. Giving does not impoverish Him. He always gives. The "unspeakable gift" of His beloved Son is God's style of generosity. His scale is worthy of His greatness. He doesn't want His servants to be ill-equipped and threadbare, struggling on like Bob Cratchit for Scrooge. My visit to the lady who owned the diamond farm hammered something else into my mind. "Never compromise because of money." Don't sell your soul for a plate of red porridge.

Later on, when I felt the Lord tell me to order the first big Gospel tent, I stood there and said, "Lord, I am a poor missionary. Look, my pockets are empty!"

The Lord replied, "Don't plan with what is in your pocket, but with what is in Mine." I looked into His pockets and saw that they were full. I said, "Lord, if You allow me to plan with what is in Your pockets, then I will plan like a millionaire."

I then began to do so, literally.

184

I've found that God is as rich as He said—and as good. To Him be glory! While doing His perfect will I can ask God, not just for a loaf of bread, but for the whole bakery. His servants don't have to scramble for a piece of the pie, or fight over the crumbs. God's shop window is full of cakes.

Twelve Baskets Full

Tests? Trials of faith? They will come. They come to all of us. One morning I was sitting on the side of my bed in Malawi. I had a three-dollar-a-day room in a Baptist hostel. In fact, I was sitting down because a shock had just hit me. An urgent phone call from my office in Frankfurt had brought me horrible news. We were hundreds of thousands of dollars in the red!

At the beginning of that year, the Lord had assured me it would be a year of twelve full baskets—a basket for each month. But the baskets had never been so empty. I couldn't see how we could be in debt. I thought we had been meeting all the bills.

"Lord," I said, "why? You said there would be full baskets. But they are all empty. How can that be?"

In such moments, the Lord opens our eyes. He instructed me and said, "Remember, the baskets of the disciples were filled only *after* the multitudes had eaten. Keep on feeding the multitudes with My word and I will see to filling the baskets."

I was amazed. The divine wisdom made sense. I said, "Lord, I will do what You say, and I know You will do what You say."

Then I remembered that we were hundreds of thousands of dollars behind. It seemed beyond reason. But God reasons differently. The baskets stayed empty for twenty-four hours, and then came the news that God had filled them again. The year ended without debt. We just kept on feeding the multitudes with the Word of God, and the Lord just kept handing the supplies to us.

When we are breaking the Bread of Life to the spiritually starving, God cannot let us down. That year, we saw 1.5 million precious people respond to the call of God to be saved in our CfaN African crusades alone.

Not A Bootlace the World's Way

The plan of God is spelled out clearly in the Bible. We see it in the familiar story about Abraham and Lot. Lot, the nephew of Abraham, had been carried off by Chedorlaomer after a battle against five kings. One of the defeated kings was the king of Sodom. Abraham, with some confederates, went to the rescue and recovered everything Chedorlaomer had taken, including the captives.

The king of Sodom then started to tell Abraham what to do with the spoils. "You keep all the goods and I will keep the persons," he said. That was the whole idea in those days. One country pillaged another, like parasites. But now the king of Sodom was in for a surprise. Abraham replied:

> I have lift up my hand unto the Lord, the most high God, the possessor of heaven and earth, that I will not take from a thread even to a shoelatchet, That I will not take any thing that is thine, lest thou shouldest say, I have made Abram rich. (Gen. 14:22–23)

That king had come up against something new in the world. Abraham was a man with a new way of life—faith in God. He was one of God's VIPs. In his hands, he held a blueprint for a city "whose builder and maker is God" (Heb. 11:10). The way of the world was finished for Abraham. He had handed over his life to God. He was now the Lord's personal responsibility. Abraham had the Word and the promise of the almighty God.

Then God said to Abraham "I am thy exceeding great reward" (Gen. 15:1). Later, we discover that "the Lord had blessed Abraham in all things" (Gen. 24:1). All things! That is Bible language, not the world's. Here are more examples (with emphasis added):

How shall he not . . . give us a*ll things?* (Rom.8:32)

All things are yours. (1 Cor. 3:21)

Your heavenly Father knows that you need *all these things*. . . . *All these things* shall be added unto you. (Matt. 6:32–33, NKJV)

His divine power hath given unto us *all things*. (2 Pet. 1:3)

That is the Abraham way. Be a child of Abraham! Trust God to the uttermost. He cannot and will not fail.

18
History on the Rope

The eyes of Jesus seem to look at me from behind the lines of print in my Bible, as a face peering through a lattice. Across the years I have not only learned to look for His face as I read the Word, I yearn for it. I cannot interpret the words unless His face is behind the lines of print. Because of His presence when I read the Bible, I am often "there"—in the scene. It is as if I am walking the dusty paths behind a herd of sheep with Abraham, clambering over rocks in battle with David, or sitting in Galilee as Jesus talks to the group around me. Because of Jesus the Bible is alive to me— a "living Word."

That was my experience one morning when I picked up the Bible and read the following passage:

> And David was then in an hold, and the garrison of the Philistines was then in Bethlehem.
>
> And David longed, and said, Oh that one would give me drink of the water of the well of Bethlehem, which is by the gate!
>
> And the three mighty men brake through the host of the Philistines, and drew water out of the well of Bethlehem, that was by the gate, and took it, and brought it to David: nevertheless he would not drink thereof, but poured it out unto the Lord.
>
> And he said, Be it far from me, O Lord, that I should do this: is not this the blood of the men that went in jeopardy of their lives? therefore he would not drink it. These things did these three mighty men. (2 Sam. 23:14–17)

The Sigh and the Cry for Water

The particular well David had in mind was renowned for its clear, fresh water. There was but one problem: it was situated behind enemy lines. The Philistines held it. Standing near, within earshot as David spoke his inner wish out loud, were several of his best warriors. To them, David's wish was their command. Three of them looked at one another, nodded their heads into instant partnership and said, "Let's go."

They knew the dangers. They might have to pay for David's cup of water with their lifeblood. But they never hesitated, protested, or complained. They had but one mission in life: to please their commander. Even though David would have never sent them on such a difficult mission for such a trivial thing, they were eager to go, because David was their lord. They knew his mind, and that was enough. Risks were their common duty. Loyalty does not wait for orders. Hesitation would suggest they were reluctant to please their leader.

David's wish for a drink of water brings to mind the similar, but far more important, words of Jesus as He hung on the cross: "I thirst!" Although His thirst was physical also, it reached far beyond that. His great thirst was for the salvation of men and women. It was that thirst which brought Him to earth and sent Him to the cross. His physical thirst was only the result of His infinite desire for the souls of His creatures.

That cry from the cross—"I thirst"—rings in our ears forever. What pathos, what power is contained in those two words. Unless it is felt—and repeated—by His followers today, the world will remain unsaved.

From a wish that was little more than a whim, David's men set out to please him. They could have brought water from a safer place. They could have even told him it was from the well at Bethlehem and he probably would not have known the difference. But that would not have satisfied their sense of utter devotion to their lord. When it came to serving their master they did not count their lives dear.

Every time I read that story I am challenged. How many of us would be as ready to act similarly for our Lord Jesus? We know His desire—the salvation of souls. Why then should we need urgings and commands before we acknowledge it? Simple knowledge of His thirst should inspire us to action. The desires of the Son of God—what could be a louder call? If David's men put their lives to risk to fulfill the inner desire of their commander, how much more should we strive to fulfill the divine desires of the Master who has died for us and given us eternal life? So what if there is danger involved? We have something David's men did not have—the promise of God's power, protection, and provision as we fulfill the wish of His Son.

The Well of Bethlehem

The well of Bethlehem was surrounded by enemy troops. But David's three warriors took their swords, along with their water vessel, and began their exploit. The well was sunk very deep into the ground, which increased the danger involved. The precious waters were deep down, yet this was the water David longed for. Somebody had to go down and bring it up.

What a vivid picture of our present situation! Multitudes who are in the depths of darkness have to be reached. They must be brought up to the light. Whole nations are in spiritual graves. Somebody has to go down and do the job. The well of Bethlehem was in Philistine hands. This meant that the warriors first had to break through enemy lines. There was a skirmish, then a breakthrough. Yet those three men were driven and strengthened by their determination to please their commander-in-chief.

Holding the Rope

A mideastern well normally has some mechanical means to bring the water to the surface. But suppose this was not the case? The Philistines may have, as they often did, cut the rope or removed the pulley which would have been used to draw water from the well. Those three men were faced with a difficult, almost impossible task when they arrived at the well. First they had to organize—determine who should go down into the well. While one went down on a rope, the others would have to hold him.

As I look at this process I see it as the only way when it comes to world evangelism. Teamwork is absolutely essential. World outreach today needs, and always has needed, those who are willing to go down and those who are willing to hold the rope—the support line of the ones who have gone down. Those who hold it, however, are just as important as those who go down. The supporters dare not slacken their hold on the rope until the man with the water is all the way up. That rope is a lifeline. Any relaxation of grip, and the man depending on the others is lost.

Those who go out at the desire of Jesus, in order to bring Him the water He longs for, are in exactly the same position. Without the rope holders (the supporters), tragedy would take place.

Logistics

God takes it most seriously when anyone in any church says that we should cut back on our commitment to world evangelism. To slacken our hands on the rope of support for those who have risked so much for the task is to fail God. Too much depends on their efforts. The missionaries themselves depend on that lifeline of financial and prayer support. More important, the whole Gospel project of Christ—spreading the good news—depends on our constant and increasing support.

These are kingdom-of-God logistics. I praise God for the men and women who back us with money, prayer, and intercession, thus keeping the tension on the rope. I remember many days when I have been in the darkness of a well in some place across the world. I knew God wanted me to go down and bring Him up water. In that well I have felt the presence of the hosts of hell. Yet every time I knew there were faithful prayer partners who held the rope and stood with me night and day. Thank God for these rope holders!

Eventually, the warrior on the end of the rope was pulled out of the well. In his hands was the container with the precious water. All three men rejoiced and immediately began their journey back home. I can imagine the two flanked the one carrying the precious water—protecting him, making certain he did not stumble, looking out on all sides for enemy snipers. How carefully the warrior carried the vessel. Under no circumstances did he want to lose one drop of what he had gone to fetch. The men on each side had their swords in their hands and were opening the way for the middle man. It was perfect teamwork. No one was more important than the other. All were needed.

Likewise, the kingdom of God depends so much upon the union of Holy-Ghost anointed ministries. Evangelism and missions require the sum total of all efforts. "Like a mighty army moves the church of God," we sing. But this needs to be a reality if we are to fulfill the Great Commission.

Heroes

The warriors finally arrived at the tent of David, their lord, with the water and their blood-stained swords. But he did a strange thing: He refused to drink the water! He realized that they had risked their very blood to bring it to him—not just the one who brought the cup in his hands, but all three were heroes. Some might have honored only the one who went down into the well, but not so with David. All three warriors had a vital part in this victory.

One day we will kneel before our heavenly Father. All God's children will be there—those who went down into the pits, as well as those who held the ropes faithfully. I am sure that we will witness many great surprises. Those who had been so inconspicuous will, all of a sudden, be heroes in the kingdom of heaven. Their reward will be great. The Lord may not say "much done" but "well done, thou good and faithful servant" (Matt. 25:21).

A Janitor Hero

A pastor in Germany told me of one old lady in his church whose job it was to clean the church building after use. One day she came to him and said she had had a wonderful dream, that she stood before the gate of eternity. Many people were lined up, and she joined them. Then she realized that all the people in front of her held sheaves in their arms, while she presented only a few stalks of wheat. She felt very uncomfortable and let others, who came behind her, get in front. Then the gate was flung open. Her name was called. It was the Lord. Trembling, she stepped forward with those pitiful stalks in her hand. But the Lord spoke to her those marvelous words from the Book of Matthew: "You have been faithful over few, I will put you over much." Then she woke up.

The pastor told me that exactly a week after this dream the lady died. I was deeply touched. Holding the rope is not always glamorous, but it surely is worthwhile.

Although the pit is deeper and darker than ever, the promise of God is we will be more productive than ever—if we work hand-in-hand with each other. God is faithful. If we are to fulfill the Word of the Lord, we must be ready to go down to the lost, or else be ready to keep our hands firmly grasping the supporting rope.

History on the End of a Rope

The men from David's army were not the only ones who held onto ropes. Jeremiah the prophet was pulled from a pit where the enemy had thrown him to die. Although Joseph's brothers threw him into a pit, it was at the secret initiative of their eldest brother, Reuben, that he was pulled out. His rescue eventually prevented famine in that ancient world. When Paul needed to escape from the city of Damascus, there were men who risked their lives to let him down over the city wall in a huge basket so he could escape. All these helpers only grasped ropes, yet they all held the future in their hands.

Suppose Joseph had been left in the pit—what would have happened to Egypt and to Jacob's family, as well as to a future son of Jacob, our Lord Jesus?

Suppose Jeremiah had not been rescued, and that his work had perished with him in that horrible pit. Would we have had his prophecies, and would Israel have, through these long centuries, drawn the comfort and hope which was theirs through his words? A world without any memory of Jeremiah, without his wonderful books in the Bible, would be a poorer world indeed. But somebody held the rope, and Jeremiah was rescued.

194

Suppose the apostle Paul had not escaped those seeking to assassinate him, or that his rope holders had let his basket crash and kill him! He was the man who brought Christianity to Europe. If they had known that the destinies of nations dangled on the end of that one little rope, how much tighter might they have gripped it. But they held on strongly enough, and we owe those nameless believers eternal thanks.

I am convinced in my heart that those who are rope holders in world evangelism today are making history for time and eternity. Can you feel the pull? Do you hear the multitudes calling upon the name of the Lord for salvation? Do you see that massive exodus from the kingdom of darkness into the marvelous light of God? These precious souls saved are the future citizens of the New Jerusalem. We cannot afford to reduce our global efforts to bring the Gospel of salvation to the nations. We dare not do less than we are doing. Instead, we must do far more. Too much is at stake. The eternity of millions depends on what we do *today*.

19
Integrity: The Satanic Target

When I was a young minister, I attended a pastors' conference where there was great blessing. One afternoon as we were praying, the power of God fell, and we all, to the man, dropped to our knees before the Lord. An elderly servant of God in his nineties knelt next to me; He was praying with such earnestness that I couldn't help but hear. I opened my eyes to watch and listen. This is what he prayed: "Lord, forgive me where I have allowed things into my life and ministry that were not clean. . . ."

His prayer moved me deeply. I found myself following with a prayer of my own. "Lord, help me, please. May I never allow anything unclean in my life and ministry. Help me so that, when I am old, I need not pray a prayer like my precious brother has prayed."

This is the Word of the Lord to all who want to minister for him: *You must mind in the beginning what matters in the end!* You carry the souls of many in your hands. Walk circumspectly.

Satanic Strategy

Christians who are at the forefront are prime targets for Satan— and for attacks of the media, as well. Neither the devil nor the press are shining examples of accuracy or mercy. Satanic hatred has scored off of some of God's servants lately. The tragedies of sin have been welcome copy to the scandal sheets, which covered the indiscretions with full orchestration. David wrote a poetic lament mourning the death of his mortal foe, King Saul. But modern writers are smaller men, of less nobility and civilization. They often maximize the damage to the kingdom of God.

I am writing this chapter to put you on your guard. The devil is very patient. He is implacable. Hell will brood and plot for years, engineering circumstances. Demon powers will try every devious means to encompass and destroy a believer's testimony. The devil is a full-time professional opponent. Christ repulsed him, but, biding his time, Satan then attacked the disciples (Luke 22:31). Judas betrayed Jesus; Peter denied Him with oaths and curses; and the rest forsook the Lord and fled during His crisis hour (Matt. 26:56). Incredible!

The enemy often lulls us into a sense of false immunity. He allows us to resist mild temptations, deceiving us about our moral strength. Then Satan turns his big guns on our unguarded flanks—just where we thought we were so strong!

Guard your "strong" points! We often despise those who fall, which is a way of drawing attention to our own superior holiness. Remember—better men have fallen than we are. Never underestimate satanic subtlety. Only saving grace preserves our feet from slipping.

If you consider spiritual warfare, remember that its main battleground is in your own heart and mind, not up in the skies somewhere. "Keep thy heart with all diligence; for out of it are the issues of life" (Prov. 4:23). Before you go into combat daily, "Watch and pray, that ye enter not into temptation" (Matt. 26:41).

Right at the start, make a covenant with God to live a holy life. But remember that determination alone will not do it. Success, in and of yourself, is not guaranteed, even with a contract written with a pen dipped in your very blood.

A Celestial Example of Perfect Service

The Bible says God "is able to keep us from falling" (Jude 24). But how?

How can we serve perfectly? A key is found in Isaiah 6:1–3.

In the year that King Uzziah died I saw also the Lord sitting upon a
throne, high and lifted up, and his train filled the temple.

Above it stood the seraphims: each one had six wings; with twain he
covered his face, and with twain he covered his feet, and with twain he
did fly.

And one cried unto another, and said, Holy, holy, holy, is the Lord of
hosts: the whole earth is full of his glory.

Seraphs are throne angels of the Most High. Nothing sullied
would be allowed so close to God and the seat of all power in heaven,
on earth, and under the earth. Isaiah saw these celestial intelligences
serving the Lord in the holiest place of all, the atmosphere of God's
immediate presence. Somewhere here is a challenge to purity, along
with the way to achieve it. These creatures are our models.

The noticeable feature about these seraphs is that they each had
six wings. Two wings covered their faces showing they were humble.
Two wings covered their feet showing they were pure. They used two
wings to fly around the throne. They were creatures of worship and
praise.

Humility

Why did these mighty beings cover their glorious and beautiful
faces and prevent the young prophet Isaiah from seeing them? It was
to keep him from looking on them—which might have prevented
him from seeing the Lord. The seraphs would not "upstage" the
Lord and distract Isaiah's gaze from the throne. Notice, also, that
though they were the most holy of creatures themselves, they only
spoke of the holiness of the Lord and of His glory. Humility is part of
holiness.

The same lesson comes from the Mount of Transfiguration (Matt.
17:1–8). In those marvelous moments on the slopes of Mt. Herman
where Jesus had gone with Peter, James, and John, Moses and Elijah
appeared. However, even though these men appeared in shining
clothes, they quickly faded, and soon the disciples saw Jesus only.
The Father's interest was similar. He did not talk to the disciples

about the two great prophets of Israel. The Father spoke to the disciples and said, "This is my beloved Son, in whom I am well pleased; hear ye him."

Jesus Christ, the Son of God, is the center focus of all our worship. Every miracle comes from Him. What room is there for human pride? These heavenly seraphs, princes of glory burning like flames, hid their own attractions. Moses and Elijah, appearing in their glory, were giants among redeemed mortals. Yet they quickly retired into the background so that only Jesus would be seen. How much more should we fragile and fading earth folk give Him all the glory.

Here lies a spiritual risk for all servants of the Lord. Are we working for recognition, to make a name for ourselves? Does an evangelist want a "big meeting" just to use the tens of thousands of people for a backdrop to highlight his own ego or imagined greatness? The light from the cross is not the limelight for any preacher! Jesus Christ did not die to give us a career, but to save the lost!

Any Christian who aims to dazzle dims God's glory. Any preacher who preaches for personal admiration will draw people who see only himself—and not God. The greatest preacher in history, the apostle Paul, said, "For though I preach the gospel, I have nothing to glory of: for necessity is laid upon me; yea, woe is unto me, if I preach not the gospel!" (1 Cor. 9:16).

Examining the character of John the Baptist should lead us to a sobering view of ourselves. He was of such stature that some wondered if he was the Messiah himself. Even Christ said John was the greatest born of woman. When more people began to turn to Christ than were following John's ministry, John's followers were jealous. But not John. He told them that Jesus must increase, and "I must decrease." When half the nation came, he pointed away from himself to Jesus. At the river he pointed to Jesus and cried, "Behold the Lamb of God!" Every single thing that John said about himself was a declaration of his own lowliness. Greatness begins and ends with humility. That is what it means to cover one's face.

The Lord is a jealous God. "My glory will I not give to another" (Isa. 42:8). To be proud in the presence of the King of kings is to touch the very ark of God, a sin for which Uzzah died (2 Sam. 6:6–7).

Herod puffed up like a bullfrog sitting on a lily pad when the crowd shouted that he was a god. But God would not allow him to share the glory, and struck him down. "Because he gave not God the glory: and he was eaten of worms," a terrible disease known by doctors today (Acts 12:23).

Those privileged to exercise the gifts of the Spirit must be especially careful. Showoffs will be shown up. Spiritual gifts are not Oscars for display, won as trophies of performance. Don't decorate yourself ostentatiously with God's power tools. Don't make tiaras, necklaces, and rings from the spiritual gifts for your own adornment. The sentry of your heart's door is called "Humility." Dismiss that guardian and the unprotected gate is soon battered in, with the enemy taking over.

Purity Is Next to Probity

The second pair of wings covered the seraphs' feet, signifying purity. The cleanest man makes contact with the ground as he walks. There was no dust near the throne, of course, but the seraphs' act was symbolic. It signaled the need to walk in holiness before the Lord. Jesus made a special point of this when He stooped to wash the feet of the disciples. Such cleansing was needed. He said, "He that is washed needeth not save to wash his feet, but is clean every whit" (John 13:10).

First, we must watch where we walk. Paul said we should make no preparation for the works of the flesh. Don't pray "Lead us not into temptation," and then deliberately walk toward it. Unclean feet are the symbol of a careless walk. "Be ye clean, that bear the vessels of the Lord" (Isa. 52:11).

Unfortunately, such advice is more easily given than taken. The modern media pour moral pollution into the atmosphere, like chimneys belching soot. We need a gas mask to keep from breathing in the soul diseases of a materialistic age with its accompanying unbelief. It is a tough world in which to live.

Our best safeguard is to use the Word constantly to wash our minds. Our thought life, conditioned by the Word of God and the covering of the blood of Jesus, is impregnable. Peter told us to "Gird up the loins of your mind" (1 Pet. 1:13). That is best done by a daily reading of the Word. It is an immunization injection against all spiritual infections. As David wisely said, "Thy word have I hid in my heart, that I might not sin against thee" (Ps. 119:11). Scientists have produced a polish for cars which simply rejects dirt. Long before such scientific developments, however, believers found that the power of the Word repulses sin.

How can we do what Scripture says, when it directs us to focus on "Whatsoever things are . . . lovely" (Phil. 4:8)? To begin with, the Bible gives us things that are lovely to think on, as well as fortifying to our desires and motives. Pray also, "lead us not into temptation." Then never go where temptation will be your biggest problem.

It is possible, I have discovered, to stand before men with an open countenance on any platform, my motives transparent, with no shame to conceal. It is an experience that is worth everything. Better still, you can have confidence as you stand before God. We read in Genesis of Esau selling his birthright for a bowl of pottage; similarly, a whole generation of Israel lost the Promised Land and died in the wilderness because they yearned for the cucumbers of Egypt. Don't lose everything for a passing pleasure. God warned Israel that they would receive the fruit of their thoughts, a terrible warning which eventually came to pass.

Worship and Praise

The seraphs used their third pair of wings to fly. And as they flew, they cried out, saying, "Holy, holy, holy, is the Lord of hosts: the whole earth is full of his glory" (Isa. 6:3). They flew and sang. That was worship! The beat of their wings was music.

It needs to be pointed out that these heavenly beings didn't cry, "Love, love, love," or "Peace, peace, peace." Rather they sang, "Holy, holy, holy is the Lord of hosts." The highest zenith of praise and the highest form of worship is always connected with the holiness and glory of God.

How could these angels say that the whole earth is full of God's glory? Had they never heard of heathen and atheistic empires, of war, hatred, greed, and suffering? Yes, of course they had. However, they saw them from a higher viewpoint as they flew before the throne. They had God's perspective, not the human view. Soaring above the earthly scene, the total situation revealed, they burst into rapturous exclamation. Scanning horizons beyond the sight of earth dwellers, the skies of all tomorrows, they sang, "the whole earth is full of his glory."

We need to get the "throne perspective." What is your angle of looking? Have you a molehill aspect or the Mount Everest view? Are you a flatlander with a two-dimensional outlook? Or do you dwell on the spiritual highlands where God's dimension clears your outlook?

You ascend to God's throne when you praise and worship. Praise lifts you. Doubt and murmuring, instead of wings of song, are iron boots on your feet. In worship we contemplate the throne, the power of the Lord, and His holiness. There we rest under His protection.

In the throne room Isaiah was equipped, sent, and cleansed with the altar fire in order to be God's servant with perfect integrity. When we serve the Lord with purity of motive, rejoicing in His presence before His throne, we are invincible, impregnable. Trouble starts when we lose the throne perspective. But elevated by worship to the third dimension, our character will be armor-plated.

The Second Key: An Earthly Example

I am writing out the following Scripture to be sure you will read it. Ponder it carefully and reverently. Let the Holy Spirit burn it into your soul.

> Behold, here I am: witness against me before the Lord, and before his anointed: whose ox have I taken? or whose ass have I taken? or whom have I defrauded? whom have I oppressed? or of whose hand have I received any bribe to blind mine eyes therewith? and I will restore it to you. (1 Sam. 12:3)

This bold challenge was part of the farewell speech of Samuel before Israel. The Judges Period of Israel ended with Samuel, who was by far the finest of these charismatic deliverers. His words, which I have quoted here, are, for their times, amazing.

In those early days, petty oppressions were regarded as simply a ruler's perks. Sheer tyranny surprised no one. For Samuel to be able to make a public challenge of his own probity gives him a stature unequaled among the world's leaders. Samuel's duty to govern and to deal with wrongdoers was absolute, and his judgments were without appeal. Those upon whom he had imposed penalties could have held a grudge against him and been very vindictive. His public words would have given them their opportunity. They could have spoken and claimed that he had done them ill.

A Prototype to Follow

What happened? Samuel's reputation was so high that he had no fear. The massed representatives of the nation roared out, "Thou hast not defrauded us, nor oppressed us, neither hast thou taken ought of any man's hand" (1 Sam. 12:4). He had judged all and now all judged him innocent, an unflawed man of God. A genuine prototype to follow.

Samuel had never taken a bribe or advantage on one single occasion for a period of a half-century or more. Such behavior did not come only from being scrupulously thoughtful. In the heat of the moment, such restraint is not always possible. His heart was right, and that was his secret. Honesty had become his natural instinct as a man filled with God and with God's Word. Even when he had no time to consider, and was acting automatically, he never put a foot wrong.

However, the unanimous testimony of Israel was not enough for Samuel. He knew that some of the people, in fact sometimes all the people, can be fooled—impressed by a mere pose. For Samuel, only one judgment really mattered, that of the Lord's. We read, "Samuel called unto the Lord; and the Lord sent thunder and rain that day: and all the people greatly feared the Lord and Samuel" (1 Sam. 12:18).

The signs from the sky meant God thundered His endorsement of His servant. It was harvest time—the dry season. But when the Lord's anointed prophet raised his arms and asked for heaven's vote, a miracle happened. The sky quickly filled with clouds and then came lightning, thunder, and rain. This was God's "Amen," approving Samuel's integrity.

The people crouched in awe before such a supernatural display. God had exposed the heart of Samuel to them all. Throughout the humdrum, everyday duties and affairs of the people, Samuel always had acted with rectitude. In his handling of money and every small judgment and decision, when nobody would have seen, there had never been a bad or rotten deal.

Now God brought it to light and sealed it. Moreover, God gave a revelation of what it meant. He was with Samuel, and He and this man were as one. Samuel shared the greatness of the Lord, so that the very heavens responded to testify. Shady dealings, along with petty and sordid tricks, had no place in Samuel's record. Samuel's honesty linked him with the authority of God.

That which is impure and shabby puts us outside the realm of the Spirit. God Himself will approve us when we keep both feet within the kingdom of God. Power, glory, and blessing will show earthly desire to be a murky shadow. The Almighty Himself embraces the cause of a man who can stand up and declare his integrity before the whole world, unafraid to ask the "Samuel questions." The time to begin these godly practices is right now, at the beginning of one's ministry, not after having learned these truths by bitter experience. Even if you have sinned in this area, you can begin living in integrity right now.

The Third Key: Anointed Footsteps

"It is like the precious ointment upon the head, that ran down upon the beard, even Aaron's beard: that went down to the skirts of his garments" (Ps. 133:2). What an anointing—so copious! That sacred oil flowed down his robes and dripped onto his feet and onto the floor. The ointment was specially prepared for the High Priest alone, and it carried its own unique perfume. Wherever Aaron walked, the oil on his feet and that which still dripped from the skirts of his garments marked his movements. People could easily recognize his footsteps as those of the high priest.

May God grant, that even after we have left this world, we shall leave behind anointed footsteps for generations to come. The anointing of God upon you gives you the walk of Aaron. These memories of integrity in a man of God are better than an inscription on the finest marble. Anointed men and women make history, which is everlasting in the kingdom of God.

20

Battering Rams of Intercession

The privileged evangelist is the one who has intercessors behind him. Intercessors are the munition workers providing the dynamite for our Gospel bombardment of hell. Intercessors are more than prayer partners, they are "Moses people."

Moses was an intercessor. As an Egyptian prince, he was trained in the science of warfare. He may have even commanded soldiers. But when Israel's existence was threatened, Moses left the fighting to others and gave himself to intercessory prayer. He defended his people by pleading their cause with God.

Forty years earlier, Moses had taken things upon himself while trying to deliver Israel. Incensed over the way his enslaved people were being treated, he struck the first blow for their freedom. He killed an Egyptian taskmaster. But instead of making things easier for the Hebrew people, he made things even worse—and was forced to flee into the desert.

At the end of his career, he again asserted himself in a way which the Bible describes as unbelief. The discontent of the people he had led out of bondage pushed him to extremes. They were thirsty, for water was scarce in the northern Sinai. During a period of despair God told him to "speak to the rock" and it would bring forth water. Instead, he stood and arrogantly upbraided the complaining people, saying, "Listen, you rebels, must we bring you water out of this rock?" (Num. 20:10,NIV). Then in a fit of rage he struck the rock with his staff. Water came forth, as it had earlier when he had used the same method. But God removed him from leadership. He had exceeded his authority and forsaken his secret.

The world has its techniques to sway the masses. Great crowds gather in our services. But I never use the unworthy methods of crowd psychology or the tricks of the rabble-rousers to stir their emotions. We use another, far more efficient method to get people to respond. It's the method Moses used: intercession. One of the finest examples is found in Exodus 17:8–16.

> Then came Amalek, and fought with Israel in Rephidim.
>
> And Moses said unto Joshua, Choose us out men, and go out, fight with Amalek: tomorrow I will stand on the top of the hill with the rod of God in mine hand.
>
> So Joshua did as Moses had said to him, and fought with Amalek: and Moses, Aaron, and Hur went up to the top of the hill.
>
> And it came to pass, when Moses held up his hand, that Israel prevailed: and when he let down his hand, Amalek prevailed.
>
> But Moses' hands were heavy; and they took a stone, and put it under him, and he sat thereon; and Aaron and Hur stayed up his hands, the one on the one side, and the other on the other side; and his hands were steady until the going down of the sun.
>
> And Joshua discomfited Amalek and his people with the edge of the sword.
>
> And the Lord said unto Moses, Write this for a memorial in a book, and rehearse it in the ears of Joshua: for I will utterly put out the remembrance of Amalek from under heaven.

While Joshua and the troops of Israel were in the valley fighting, Moses won the battle by intercession. Some don't pray. They call it a mystery and write off prayer. Yet they certainly make use of other things which they don't understand. Why, for instance, did the troops of Amalek prevail when Moses' arms became heavy? Prayer is not a matter of logic, but revelation. Throughout history, men have found that God answers prayer. There is no use arguing with the way things are. As long as Moses interceded for his people the battle went in their favor. When he ceased, for whatever reason, the enemy surged ahead. That's how it happens, not only in the desert of the Sinai, but in many other Biblical tories. Intercession changes things.

Reaching the Heart of God

What are the principles of intercession, so necessary in changing the world? Again we find the answers in the life of Moses.

Intercession began in Moses' heart. It's interesting that in recording the story of Moses on the mountaintop at Rephidim, nothing is said about the words Moses spoke. His prayer was not a formal, correct litany, or a word-for-word formula. Moses may not have *said* anything, but as Paul wrote to the Romans more than a thousand years later, the Holy Spirit prayed through him with "groaning which cannot be uttered" (Rom. 8:26). The only way Moses could express this was by lifting his hands.

Aaron and Hur shared in this victory by supporting his arms. The heart of God is not necessarily reached by sounds from our lips. God looks upon our heart. Yet the human emotion and body cries out to express itself. Moses put himself into his supplications physically. The apostle Paul wrote, "I want men everywhere to lift up holy hands in prayer" (1 Tim. 2:8, NIV). Moses' intensity was too great for mere words, yet, as with us all, it is virtually impossible to plead in silence.

Just a few sentences before, in his letter to young Timothy, Paul had touched on this when he urged "supplications, prayers, intercessions, and giving of thanks, be made for all men" (1 Tim. 2:1). That's going to require some kind of expression. With Moses it was physical, as he lifted his hands before God and in behalf of his people.

Battering Rams of Intercession

I love the story of Moses at Rephidim. One man lifted his hands, but two men helped him do so. Much has been written about the need for men "to stand in the gap," but the years pass and who can point to such a man? Abraham interceded for Sodom but was unsuccessful. His prayer was futile, for the Sodomites did not want to be saved. Moses, on the other hand, was successful in his intercession for the Israelites, not only because they cooperated with God by fighting in the valley below, but because others joined him in the task of intercession. In fact, this story shows we cannot leave the praying to one man or to one woman—or to a few so-called prayer warriors. It is the mandatory task of many. Let the millions gather to storm the citadel of sin!

In our CfaN Gospel crusades, we follow this principle. Suzette Hattingh is a vital member of the CfaN team. Much of what I'm writing in this chapter must be credited to her. Suzette does far more than sign up prayer partners. She gathers together thousands, instructing and leading them in true intercession. They do far more than sing a few choruses and pray for a blessing; they are busy pulling down the strongholds of Satan. Intercessors are mighty battering rams.

In our intercession meetings we are not bothered with finding the right words to say, but with the expression of the heart. Intercessors in our meetings may kneel, sit, stand, lie down before the Lord, or walk around. There is no waiting while some pastor pleads, "Someone please lead us in prayer." Instead, everyone prays together, just as those early disciples did in the Book of Acts. There is liberty, but no license; freedom, but no extravagance. Every gathering must have order and respect. But we are not afraid of people calling upon God and crying out to Him, even with tears.

Touch-Point on Earth of Heavenly Power

Amalek attacked Israel with satanic hostility, and that enmity was met by the spiritual forces of prayer. There was no reason for Amalek to attack. The Israelites were just passing through that region on their way to Mount Sinai, several miles down the path. The followers of Amalek lived in the region of Rephidim. It would have been easy to step aside and let the Israelites pass by and be gone. But the very presence of the people of God stirred the demons and caused the Amalakites to react with frenzied hostility. Their assault literally was devil-inspired and quite irrational. Only spiritual power could resist it.

The same situation exists today. The enemies of the Gospel walk "according to the prince of the power of the air, the spirit that now worketh in the children of disobedience" (Eph. 2:2). This is the spirit of the age. We must come to grips spiritually with this in order for that power to be broken. Good sermons or discussion alone will never do the job. Evil lies deep. The only way to drive it out of its burrows is all-prevailing prayer and supplication! We must enter into Calvary victory "By My Spirit," said the Lord. Intercession is like a lightning conductor, the touch-point on earth of heavenly power.

Relationship Between Prayer and Events

The tide of battle did not ebb and flow according to Joshua's strategy in the valley, but according to the intercession of the men on the mountaintop. Those who fought on the hilltop and those who struggled in the valley were one. The relationship between prayer and events was clearly demonstrated.

Suzette Hattingh says that one day she suddenly realized the five offices of the church named in Ephesians 4—apostles, prophets, evangelists, pastors, and teachers—were like fingers on a hand. Each finger functions on its own, but only when connected to the palm of a hand. That palm represents the body of Christ. Intercession is a function of the body, an assignment for all believers—not just a task of the fingers of the hand or the special gift of men whom Jesus gives to the church. All members of the body of Christ should intercede. This is the principle we employ in our crusades.

How It Is Done

Beginning about eight weeks before a crusade, Suzette involves as many members of the body of Christ as possible in intense intercession. No single champion prays alone, but instead the whole church puts its weight behind the onslaught. The gates of hell are stormed, and we knock on the doors of heaven in supplication. We do this expressly for the salvation of souls and the moving of God's Spirit.

The intensity of such intercession does not climax and conclude when the crusade starts. It is continued right up to the altar call. Hundreds, sometimes even thousands, pray and are engaged in spiritual warfare during our crusade meetings. At the very time the evangelist is working, preaching, and ministering, those behind the scenes are dealing with spiritual forces to help obtain the evangelist's victory. It is just like Moses praying for Joshua while the latter was in

211

the thick of the battle. If intercession is not needed when the satanic onslaught is greatest, then when is it needed?

In the Bible account in Exodus 17, the two groups, Israel's army and Moses' companions, were in separate places, yet together fought the same battle at the same time. In our evangelistic meetings, the intercessors also may be away from the crusade grounds, praying in a field away from the main site or in a different hall. But these prayer warriors are an active part of the evangelistic meeting itself, upholding the evangelist and joining with the armies of heaven to push back the powers of darkness. The effectiveness of this strategy certainly has been proven. With this intercessory backing, the enemy must withdraw, leaving unconverted people open to the power of the Word of God. There is a great harvest of souls, an edification of the body of Christ and a fulfillment of the Word of God. We all thus become partners with Christ and shareholders in His harvest. Our intercessors hold back the armies of Satan until souls are safe inside the kingdom of God.

Since this strategy originated with God, it is therefore blessed by Him. It affects the individual Christian, the churches, the city, the country, and above all, the unbeliever. Intercession builds a highway for the evangelism that wins the world.

The Meaning

Just as Moses and Joshua worked together in the battle, so the Lord always intends for intercession and evangelism to function in combination. Intercession and evangelism are one in battle. They are like a hand in a glove, or water in a river bed, or branches in a vine.

Intercession that is not linked to soul-saving is like an arrow shot without a target, an athlete running a race which has no finish line, or a football game without a goal line. If we pray for revival, we should do something about it also. Intercession is preparatory work, a plow breaking up the ground for the sowing and the harvest. That does not mean we should not intercede until a crusade or similar work is arranged, but it certainly means that we should have a vision and a plan of outreach.

Then there is the other omission—evangelism without intercessory prayer. It is like cranking machinery by hand with no power supply, or fishing without a net and trying to catch the fish one by one—by the tail.

Your Rightful Inheritance

The attack by Amalek and his bandits was an attempt by the heathen to keep Israel out of their inheritance. That highlights the proper theme of intercessory effort outlined in Psalm 2:8: "Ask of me, and I shall give thee the heathen for thine inheritance, and the uttermost parts of the earth for thy possession."

Note the outline:

• We first *ask* (intercede).

• Then we *possess.*

Intercession is followed by evangelism—actually going into the land and possessing it. The same principle is found in 1 Timothy 2:1, where we are told to make intercession for all men. Intercessory prayer, however, needs a definite target. Paul states the target selected by God: "all men to be saved, and to come unto the knowledge of the truth" (1 Tim. 2:4). I thrill when I read those words "all men." The entire world can be saved through intercession and evangelism.

When we refer to the story of Moses interceding at Rephidim, we need to note that after a while he grew weary and sat down. Weariness is not a sin unless we use it as an excuse. Moses did not excuse himself by saying, "I'm tired." Sure he was tired. All men get tired. But Jesus makes it plain that weariness is never an excuse to escape His command to pray, "Men ought always to pray, and not to faint" (Luke 18:1). Tired, old Moses kept on interceding—even if that meant having to sit down on a rock and let someone hold up his hands. He was determined to pray until victory came, not until the clock said it was time for a coffee break. He knew the area of specific battle where God wanted him to fight. He was not praying in general, or fasting for no specific reason. Nor was he praying simply because he had allocated a certain time each day to pray. There was a battle raging, and he had been called by God to intercede. He was delivering a blow against a recognized enemy.

Moses did not just "say a prayer." He *travailed* in prayer, continued in prayer, persisted in prayer until Joshua had routed Amalek. It was intercession and persistence that secured the victory. Here are Suzette's definitions of travailing prayer:

- To pray that God's will be done in the world
- To intervene, mediate and work with God
- To be part of what God is doing, to serve Him in prayer
- To pray God's burden and not our own opinions. What He wants, not what we think we should pray, thereby "taking on the mind of Christ"
- To see the need for God's action and then, with boldness and confidence, to ask that He act

Definitions

Suzette points out that the word "intercession" first appears in Isaiah 53:12, where the Bible speaks of Christ who "made intercession for the transgressors." The Hebrew is *baga*, from the root meaning "to impinge with violence." "Impinge" means "to collide with." Vine's Expository Dictionary states that *baga* means "to strike up against, to be violent against, to invade, to come between, to cause to entreat, to meet with, and pray."

Baga means facing Satan in the name of Jesus on behalf of people, thereby "striking up against" and colliding with him. The word also implies travail. This is not wailing and suffering; rather it is a gentle word meaning "to come between," or to face the Father on behalf of people. Intercession, then, is made up of warfare and travail; and it contains two features: facing Satan and facing God.

Suzette also draws attention to the words for intercession used in the New Testament. One Greek word has two parts. The first means "exceeding"; the other means "to meet on behalf of or for someone's sake." In other words, it means reaching across and doing our utmost for others.

214

Another word for intercession implies "getting the ear of the King on behalf of others." That shows that close fellowship is needed.

Webster's Dictionary describes intercession as "mediation, entreaty, prayer or petition on behalf of another." The verb "intercede" is defined as "an act between parties with a view to reconciling their differences or points of contention, to mediate, to plead or to interpose on behalf of another." Entreaty, petition, plead, intervene, interpose—that is prayer raised to its highest temperature.

Phineas intervened after Israel grossly sinned and a plague broke out throughout the land. The spreading terror was checked, and it was counted to Phineas as righteousness for generations afterwards. Intercession involves being a peacemaker, bringing men and women into the peace of God. It raises a harvest of righteousness which counts for eternity. Such is the power of intercession.

Intercessory prayer needs a target—God's target. That means we must know God's concern, for He knows what is happening when we do not, and is well aware of where Satan is mustering his attack.

The Intercessor's Secrets

The Lord often gives us burdens for tasks we should do ourselves, like speaking to a person about some personal matter. The main purpose of intercession, however, is not to hear secrets about others from God. We should not go around "straightening out" the body of Christ, telling people what God thinks and sharing His confidences with everyone. (Suzette calls this "spiritual gossip" and warns that God's secrets are holy unto the Lord.) Although intercession may mean we received "messages" from the Lord for others, we have a sacred obligation to take those messages only to the person or persons God intends to have them—not to everyone. Most important, God tells us certain information so we can intercede for others, thereby bringing about the purposes He has for them. The Lord seems to share such secrets only about 2 percent of the time, however. The other 98 percent of intercession time is spent turning the world back to God as we are led by the Spirit.

Taking up the work of an intercessor is a life-changing experience, but only God can build an intercessor. If the Lord brings you through experiences which cause your heart to clamor at the throne of God for our lost world, you will not regret it—however hard the preparation work may have been.

Intercession changes your life's attitudes, bringing you a fulfillment so rich it is impossible to describe. Put your heart at God's disposal, not just your time alone, and you will have put your treasure where no moth can take hold.

Evangelism must be seen as the work of the Holy Spirit in every single sense. All aspects of an evangelistic campaign are yielded to Him—the preaching, the singing, the order of the meeting, the use of every ministry, and the gifts of the Spirit. It is one great effort, backed by local believers as well as the church at large. Evangelism removes every blockage, every hindering self-motive, and every device which may keep men from God. Evangelism is the Holy Spirit working through both intercession and ministry. Such a combination brings about the revival which is conquering the world!